Understanding Borderline Personality Disorder

How To Live Your Life, Manage Your Emotions And Heal Yourself While Living With BPD

Dr Matin Lund

Copyright © 2021 LH Press

All rights reserved. No portion of this book may be reproduced in any form without permission from the publisher, except as permitted by U.S. copyright law.

ISBN: 9798515857745

Cover by LH Press

DISCLAIMER

This book has been created to provide accurate and authoritative information regarding the subject matter covered. By sale of this book neither the publisher nor author is engaged in rendering psychological or other professional services. We advise seeking further professional medical help from a doctor.

ABOUT THE AUTHOR

A medical doctor by profession, lifelong writer by passion. Having spent time living in both the US and Pakistan Dr Matin Lund's expertise lies with Psychiatry, Psychopharmacology, Human Behavior, and Medicine. His goal is to transform how we live our lives through self-help, creating up to date content backed by science and many years of research. Presenting difficult concepts in a simple, engaging and informative way.

Apart from medicine, Dr Matin Lund has a keen interest in meditation, yoga and spirituality and also loves to travel.

SPECIAL BONUS!

Want this bonus book for FREE?!?!

51 ways to manage your emotions!

Get exclusive access to this FREE book and all of our future releases by joining our fanbase!

CONTENTS

1	Introduction	Pg 1
2	BPD Symptoms	Pg 4
	Fear of Abandonment	Pg 5
	Unstable Relationships	Pg 9
	Fluctuating Self-Image	Pg 11
	Impulsive/Self-Destructive Behavior	Pg 14
	Self-Harm/Suicidal Behavior	Pg 19
	Extreme Emotional Mood Swings	Pg 22
	Chronic Feelings of Emptiness	Pg 24
	Explosive Anger	Pg 28
	Feeling Suspicious/Out of Touch with Reality	Pg 31
3	Helping Yourself and Others	Pg 35
4	Power of the Mind	Pg 43
5	Stability	Pg 54
6	Creating an Identity	Pg 67
7	Extremes of BPD	Pg 73
8	Personal Relationships	Pg 79
9	Stress Management	Pg 85
10	Conclusion	Pg 96

CHAPTER 1
INTRODUCTION

As you may already be aware, Borderline Personality Disorder (BPD) is a mental illness associated with behavioral instability due to unhinged emotions. It is morbidity associated with other co-morbid conditions and often confused with other mental illnesses, such as Bipolar Disorder.

This book is to help you identify BPD and the thought process that goes on in the mind of someone living with it. If you are reading this book, chances are you have already been diagnosed with BPD. Or you may be merely curious about the disorder. If you are an individual who has been diagnosed with BPD, you can recommend this book to the ones close to you and share your voice and struggles with them. Or you can recommend this book to a family member or a friend suffering from this particular condition to help them with their struggles.

Mental health conditions often instill fear in people's

hearts and make them believe that it will hold them back, but that is further from the truth. You should first relax and realize that nothing terrible will befall you, especially since there is help available. In this info space-riddled era, the internet has tons of resources and accounts of people with similar struggles, proving that you are not alone!

We are currently living in an era where psychiatric medicine has progressed immensely and can help you achieve the best results. So please, do not treat your diagnosis with a sense of doom. However, with the internet, you may also be bombarded with a plethora of knowledge that is not always organized well enough or may even be too dull to be read. In this book, the information given is concise, up to date, and engaging to not bore you with just jotted facts. The vocabulary is simple and accompanied by many suggested tasks to help the readers and allow them to track or gauge their progress not to lose motivation.

You can refer to each chapter for particular sets of information during your recovery. Be aware that no amount of just reading will help. Being here is a sign of progress, but you must supplement your knowledge with consistency, patience, accountability, determination, and the desire to better yourself because you owe it to yourself to do so. You have the power to change, as many already have. We will also talk about the power of the mind to show how we are equipped with the means required to alter our mental selves. Consistency and patience are critical as you will not change overnight; this is a book, not a video game cheat code. However, we cannot stress enough that you are only human; you are not perfect and may stumble, face obstacles, and that is okay! Do not deprive yourself of the pleasures of life. Feeling like things will not get better is part of the journey, but you owe it to yourself to keep believing in yourself and keep moving forward. This journey will require you to forgive yourself. Guilt will only make your life harder and pull you away from progress. Like every aspect of life, recovery is not linear in its growth; there will be ups and downs. No matter what, keep trying to perform the tasks, and you are going to be alright. Lastly, don't stop enjoying the journey. The light at the end of the tunnel does not have to exist only at the end; it can illuminate through the entirety of your journey.

This first chapter will only introduce you to BPD. In layman's terms, this is defined as an ongoing pattern of rapidly changing moods, self-image, and general behavior, which can translate to instability in relationships, how you perceive your self-worth and place in society, and marked impulsivity. These also lead to identity problems, patterns of self-harm, fear of abandonment, and escapist self-destructive behaviors. According to recent research, BPD affects 1.6-2 % of the population residing in the USA and about 10% of all psychiatric patients. The 1.6-2% mentioned above is over 5 million citizens with BPD, 75% of which happen to be women. That's a ratio of about three women to every one man.

Before we dive into the book and outline the details of BPD, it is imperative to recognize that this is a severe mental condition that requires professional help. This book is only written to help understand BPD better. It is not a means to diagnose the disorder or treat patients suffering from it. Instead, we recommend seeking professional help to determine whether a person is suffering from BPD. With that out of the way, let's move on!

CHAPTER 2
BPD SYMPTOMS

Individuals with BPD often feel alone and scared. The unstable emotions associated with the disorder increase the probability of the individuals assuming that nobody around them understands them and their hardships. It is hard to live with a mental illness, and BPD is one of the scariest ones. However, this chapter is written to reassure you that you are not alone.

Many people experience symptoms associated with BPD, but that certainly does not entail that all of them are suffering from this disorder. There are nine major BPD symptoms, and to confirm a positive diagnosis, you must exhibit at least five of them. So if you are reading this book because you wanted to check the chances of suffering from BPD, you need to tick five of these boxes. The exhibited symptoms must also be long-standing; they should have begun in your early adolescence and impact many different aspects of your life. There is a low probability of you exhibiting five out of nine of these symptoms, so we suggest you lay back and not worry about your mental health.

According to the Diagnostic and Statistical Manual of Mental Disorders, BPD can be diagnosed as early as twelve years if the symptoms are observed for at least one year. However, most diagnoses are usually made during early adulthood. These given symptoms are essential in differentiating BPD from other mental disorders; some symptoms may overlap those of other disorders, such as Dissociative Identity Disorder, which is often misdiagnosed in place of BPD.

Symptom 1: Fear of Abandonment

The most common BPD symptom people suffer from is the fear of abandonment. This is a feeling many people often experience, irrespective of whether they have BPD or not. It is a feeling of constant fear that the people you know and love will abandon you. The friends who support you may not be there for you in the future. This feeling is related to anyone you care about. This symptom triggers an intense fear of being abandoned, even by something as small as the late arrival of a loved one home from work or a co-worker complimenting the way you look. If this feeling has been persisting for a while, we suggest visiting a professional.

This symptom has severe clinical importance in its potency to induce other significant symptoms such as suicidal behavior or non-suicidal self-injury. People with BPD are often driven to exhibit an increased likelihood of trying their best to maintain dysfunctional and harmful relationships and prematurely ending supportive and positive relationships. This fear of being left alone will present itself as efforts to maintain proximity with loved ones as per fear of being left alone, even for a short time. However, in some extreme cases, the fear can also result in violent criminal-like actions, especially towards romantic partners.

People with BPD have also been reported to likely exhibit tension associated with a fear of rejection expressed in behavior. The fear warrants stalking one's partners; their distrust towards their partners and their intentions leads them to keep an eye out for any action that could prove their intention to leave. In turn, persons with BPD may invade personal space, disrespect their partner's privacy, and be unwilling to respect and maintain boundaries in their relationships. This behavior is led by their inclination to associate the innocuous actions of their partners with intentions of leaving.

The fear of rejection in BPD is further amplified due to the lack of awareness of regulating one's emotions. Ruminations are thoughts about adverse outcomes continuously associated with BPD. The worst part about this is that BPD patients do not accept the emotions they might be having. Rumination leads them to add guilt to the cycle of not getting one's emotions as well. The fear of abandonment all in all is entwined with interpersonal dysfunction, which is an essential indicator of BPD; they are unable to recognize the needs, feelings, and intentions of others.

You may have noticed either within yourself – if you have BPD - or with the people around you with BPD that they often feel insulted or humiliated, even when the other person is trying to help or give any advice. Unwanted interference may leave these people with hypersensitivity toward establishing further boundaries or any distance whatsoever, even when there is no ill will, such as when a loved one has to travel across town for work. It is essential to realize that this fear established for a reason; it is often due to neglected childhood or any other incident that scarred them with the fear of abandonment. A lot of the time, a parent's neglect is the basis of this phobia. This neglect leaves the individuals with an insecure attachment style.

You may be aware of the four attachment styles: secure, dismissive, anxious, and fearful. The names are pretty self-explanatory. Can you guess which ones are most commonly found in BPD?

Out of the four types, only two are common in BPD: the anxious type and the fearful type. People with an anxious attachment style expect constant validation from their partners, making them appear too clingy and annoying. In contrast, people with a fearful attachment style while the fearful types are plagued by self-hate and low self-esteem and are disorganized with their erratic outbursts and inability to understand other people's behavior. This adds up to their misinterpretation of efforts in social inclusion and the fear of being left out.

When you look at it from a medical perspective, interpersonal dysfunction in BPD is also aggravated by altered or low levels of Oxytocin, also known as the 'love hormone.' So abnormal Oxytocin levels may contribute to the obstacles faced in feeling constant love or attachment toward someone.

Ultimately, the extreme efforts of trying to block people from leaving your life can do just the opposite and further drive them to move on without you. Of course, that is bound to affect further your phobia and the notion that your loved ones want to abandon you.

Symptom 2: Unstable Relationships

Maybe, you are not the kind of person who clings to other people. Maybe, you are the person who falls in love with someone new every other month. You might believe that this new person will finally make you whole again, only to end up getting disappointed. Have you perhaps gone from suddenly idealizing a person to completely despising their very presence in a matter of mere days? Do not associate these questions with just romantic relationships, but most, if not all, of your relationships.

These are principle findings in relationships where either party suffers from BPD. Many people with this disorder experience extreme emotions at the start of a new relationship; they idealize every aspect of their new partner and are willing to give the relationship their all. The problem with idealization is that you may have unrealistic opinions about the person or crave validation. However, this period of idealism is followed by an intense phase of devaluation.

Devaluation is the opposite of idealization, where you may attribute extreme flaws and low worth to the very same person you once idealized. Intense fear of rejection may also trigger a devaluation phase as a response, possibly resulting in an outburst of anger or giving up on the relationship entirely. It is sad to say that both idealization and devaluation are done subconsciously and used as defense mechanisms to avoid mental stress.

The shift from idealizing to devaluing is called splitting. Splitting is the inability to regulate emotions and causing a disturbance in rational thought. For example, a person with BPD may find it hard to understand that the other person could be multi-dimensional. Instead, they resort to a black and white rationale of judgment. This extremism in thought leads to impulsive outbursts of anger or abrupt decisions such as breaking off an otherwise healthy relationship, forming unstable relationships instead.

Another symptom of BPD is the phenomenon of dichotomous thinking, where an all-or-nothing mindset of extremes prevents one from mediating in relationships, professional life, and decision making. For example, suppose you cannot maintain a healthy relationship with your co-worker; you used to idealize them once, but suddenly, you started resenting them. This random outburst of impulsivity will ruin your relationship with your co-worker and may also jeopardize your career. Impulsivity can also open a path for other people to take advantage of your intense emotions. This impulsivity can affect a person in many ways. Students may give up going to their classes because they cannot maintain class decorum, people ruin healthy relationships, their place at work, and may even lose the most significant people in their life if they do not seek help!

Symptom 3: Fluctuating Self-Image

Unstable relationships could have a severe impact on a person's self-image. While trying to attain their perfect self, people with BPD eventually ruin their persona. They may start to feel like they do not honestly know who they are supposed to be. In addition, a loss of identity could even resulting in trying to adopt someone else's personality. All these feelings point to one fact; a prominent association of BPD is the loss of identity or constant changes in your perception of who you essentially are.

Identity Disturbance is the inconsistency of identity that involves rapidly changing goals, values, and even beliefs. It also consists of a person trying to copy or borrow aspects of personality from somebody else as they struggle to maintain their sense of self. This behavior is usually induced when one tries to emulate the person they idealize during their idealization phase. Of course, loss of self can be experienced by individuals without BPD. Still, for those with BPD, it is very profound and consistent in the sense that there's a chronic pattern of trying to encapsulate someone else or change one's fundamental core values.

Before conveying what disturbed identity is, one must first understand what a stable sense of self is. A stable identity requires people to view themselves as the same persons in the past, present, and future. It involves consistency in beliefs, values, temperament, opinions, and even social roles. Thus, even when a person exhibits contradictory actions to themselves, they can still view themselves how they usually would. It is the anchor that holds a person strong in a hostile or ever-changing world. Without the anchor, you cannot have high self-esteem and cannot tackle obstacles.

According to the circumstances, people with BPD often feel like chameleons who continuously alter their core selves. These changes are most notably based on what they think other people might want or expect from them. That is why people with BPD often prioritize group identities concerning other people rather than their individuality. This may lead to high fluctuations in political values or even religious beliefs. This is also why some individuals with this disorder may be more vulnerable to peer pressure; they would go to any lengths to remain a part of a friend circle or fraternity. Again, this occurs due to their struggle with establishing healthy boundaries in their social life.

Another association with self-image is the ability to understand others and your mental state, something called Mentalizing, which becomes hard in BPD associated with Identity Disturbance. Mentalizing prevents one from intimately bonding with other individuals, thus creating rifts. In professional life, people with BPD may also find it hard to focus on one goal at a time. It can be hard to persevere or work hard to achieve a specific purpose if your convictions and motivations keep changing. Therefore, a lack of sense can affect their job and academic performance negatively.

Figuring out what a person truly wants in life might be a real challenge. When they are experiencing something, they might not even know whether it is just a phase induced by BPD or something else. But keep in mind that, people with BPD are often tied to previously abusive households where the lack of support and validation leads to a crumbled sense of self. As a result, they base their self-worth on the opinions of other people. Often the guilt and awareness of these patterns can deter patients from seeking professional help. It is essential to realize that the longer they delay seeking help, the more they might damage several aspects of their lives.

Symptom 4: Impulsive/Self-Destructive Behavior

Many BPD patients exhibit impulsive behavioral patterns. Often, their actions are conceived without proper foresight or rational thinking. As a result, impulsive behavior is often risky and inappropriate. More often than not, impulsive behavior leads to poor and undesirable outcomes that could otherwise have been avoided given the proper foresight. However, impulsivity must not be confused with compulsion; compulsion makes a person act a certain way while knowing how harmful their actions are.

In impulsivity, one seldom realizes the abnormality of their behavior and therefore acts out under the impression of normality. Impulsivity often presents as abruptly changing or canceling plans, binge eating, escalating conflict, or carelessly spending money, amongst other things. The symptoms that we discussed previously in this chapter are also a result of impulsivity. Starting anew again and again with jobs is considered impulsive behavior. Meaningless and risky sexual endeavors and relationships are viewed as impulsive behavior due to the fear of abandonment or dissatisfaction with the other persons. Joining and leaving friend groups abruptly signifies impulsivity. But the most harmful of them all would be the impulse to cut yourself. Self-harm in itself is a symptom of BPD and a very severe one at that. Self-harm will be discussed further in this chapter and later on in subsequent chapters due to its significance in causing suffering.

You cannot merely identify impulsivity in an individual and think to yourself, "Oh, they must be having Borderline Personality Disorder." That is not how the diagnosis is made. Two criteria must be met for a positive diagnosis of impulsivity associated with BPD by a doctor. The first criterion presents an impaired personality in low self-image, instability in values, goals, and opinions. The second one is an impairment of interpersonal functioning in the form of lack of empathy and inability to be intimate due to either fear of abandonment, neediness, or a lack of trust resulting from low self-esteem.

If we look at the more medical aspect of this symptom, research has identified a genetic error that relates impulsivity to BPD. Suppose you, or someone you know, have a knack for getting into plenty of unnecessary fights for the smallest of reasons or spending too much money on useless items or struggle with self-control. This behavior has been explained in previous studies. These concluded that genetic errors in your DNA (notably Chromosome 9) are linked to partial inheritability of impulsive behavior. Mutations may alter the production of neurotransmitters, known as Dopamine and Serotonin. These changes can inhibit the individual from logically, impacting the part of the brain that prevents a person from thinking things through before acting on impulse.

For obvious reasons, impulsivity can lead to problems in a person's life; the persons suffering from it could struggle financially or even get in trouble with the law. This may seem rather extreme, but the Psychology department at the Eastern Connecticut University has reported that one-third of the people diagnosed with BPD are or have been convicted of some crime, at least once in their lifetime. These crimes range from mild to extreme: from shoplifting and speed driving to domestic violence.

Intimate Partner Violence (IPV) is the inclination to inflict harm on a loved one due to outbursts of anger. Often, BPD strongly associates itself with a psychological, physical, or sexual form of violence. The most important predictors of abuse are risk-taking and suspiciousness towards the partner on the receiving end of the abuse. This attribute ties nicely in BPD since struggling with feelings of inadequacy, which leads to suspicion of infidelity, can result in extreme or violent lashing out on a partner. Thus, BPD can get you into tons of legal trouble over domestic or sexual abuse.

Unfortunately, this abuse extends not only to partners but also to children. Borderline outbursts of anger consisting of physical violence or yelling can put children in harm's way. One can also be so involved with their BPD-induced rumination or self-loathing that they neglect their children. In extreme cases, this often leads to the arrest and incarceration of the parent due to battered baby syndrome.

People with BPD either take part in crimes or turn out to be victims. It starts by engaging in impulsive and rampant sexual relationships. However, the problem with this is that the individual with BPD may feel validated at first and may even develop a strong emotional response. However, it can eventually prevent them from enjoying meaningful and healthy romantic relationships. Furthermore, by affecting this person's foresight and decision-making skills, BPD leaves them easily vulnerable to coercion into non-consensual sex, resulting in an increased number of rape victims amongst BPD patients. As if that was not bad enough, people with BPD are often diagnosed with Sexually Transmitted Infections (STIs) due to their high partner count.

As we are already talking about sexual relationships, it is essential to mention that impulsivity and identity disturbance can also change a person's sexual orientation. Heterosexual individuals with BPD are seen to engage in sex with individuals of varying sexual orientations.

In the case of teens with emerging BPD symptoms, they may often miss their compulsory attendances in educational institutes and are more prone to substance abuse as a form of escapism. This abuse can cause them trouble with the law and even stain their relationship with their parents.

Rates of alcohol and drug abuse amongst patients with BPD are incredibly high. Hence, BPD frequently co-occurs with Alcohol Use Disorder (AUD). Patients most commonly perform substance abuse with alcohol, followed by cocaine and opiate use. A study claimed that 78% of adults with BPD were involved in substance abuse during the emergence of BPD symptoms, and 63% of adults with BPD also suffered from AUD. Unfortunately, people with both BPD and AUD suffer more and are less responsive to treatment than those who only suffer from one of the disorders at a time.

Co-occurring BPD makes it less likely for an alcoholic to stay motivated or rigorous with treatment. Suicidal thoughts plague them, and impulsivity spirals into other harmful habits like gambling, binge eating, or self-harm. It has been proven that alcoholism alters the decision-making parts of the brain responsible for self-control, thereby making it even harder for BPD patients who already suffer from impulsivity and poor foresight. Another factor is that both BPD and AUD share standard histories of child neglect or abusive households; generally, the two patient records often go hand in hand. The intense emotions one may feel due to BPD can lead to high addiction to alcohol use. BPD patients that are further fuelled by fear of being abandoned, negative thinking, and guilt may want to numb themselves with alcohol or drugs. Since the two mental illnesses are shadowing their senses, they do not realize how their actions only make their condition worse.

The co-occurrence between BPD and cocaine abuse is also increasingly high due to the troubled functioning of the Endogenous Opioid System (EOS) of the body. The EOS is responsible for relieving pain and making a person feel as if they are on a high. The EOS induces a feeling stimulated by alcohol, cocaine, and opiate use, making it more likely for BPD patients to resort to substance abuse to feel normal and internally validated.

However, these substances bring to the table their own set of problems. Substance and alcohol abuse will damage a person's vital organs more than rewarding the brain with a sense of relief. And because these substances have as many harmful effects, they are also illegal. Cocaine use will not only damage your brain. It might also send you to jail.

Just because co-occurring BPD is challenging to treat, it does not mean you should not seek professional help. Do not forget that you are not the only one suffering from these problems. A more significant majority of individuals with BPD had the same dependencies as you do, but they were eventually treated. You only need to find the right doctor. Once you do, he will be able to help you in no time!

Symptom 5: Self-Harm/Suicidal Behavior

The self-harm and the suicidal behavior that accompanies BPD is one of the attributes of impulsivity. Suicidal behavior includes, but is not limited to, thinking about suicide, making suicidal threats, or even attempts to commit suicide in the past. Self-harm is considered a deliberate attempt at destruction or alteration of body parts. It is most commonly done through cutting, but it also consists of extreme scratching, burning, skin picking, hair-pulling, or even hitting oneself with fists or nails. On some occasions, some people also abuse chemicals.

It may not be easy to understand the workings of someone who physically injures themselves. People who self-harm are often very guilt-ridden and therefore secretive about their dangerous activities. For example, a child or teenager might always make sure to be covered in a long-sleeved attire or refuses to wear a swimsuit at the beach not to reveal their visible scars, burn marks, or bruises. Their trash may reveal plenty of bloody tissues, bandages, or any blood-stained items of clothing along with sharp objects, such as pieces of glass that they often collect. It can be hard to spend time with BPD patients who harm themselves as they may be highly secretive about their belongings and may spend too much time in the bathroom, either cutting themselves or trying to hide scars. In young children, self-harm is made even worse if they are further stigmatized or scolded by their parents.

If you are reading to understand better a loved one who occasionally self-harms, there is a positive outlook to all of this. Although they self-harm and may also often have re-occurring suicidal thoughts, they will rarely want to kill themselves. This behavior is termed non-suicidal self-injury

(NSSI). However, in some severe NSSI cases and further mental impulsivities, the injuries can sometimes become fatal. So make sure to pay attention to persons with self-harming tendencies.

With such severe consequences, one might ask why people even self-mutilate in the first place? It is instinctive to believe that people engage in self-mutilation to gain more attention, but that is far from the truth. Most self-cutters do so in privacy and do an excellent job of keeping their scars, bruises, and cuts hidden from other people. These individuals rarely open up about their behaviors, and their hypersensitivity to rejection further amplifies the continuous worry of their secrets being revealed. Most people that self-mutilate do so to regulate extreme internal emotions, thoughts, and memories. A person may feel devalued by someone or by the circumstances. In turn, the negative feelings can become internalized to such a degree that the only way they feel relief is through self-mutilation.

This being said, the relief that they feel is not in the sense of reduced anxiety or stress. It is more of a perceived kind that is only temporary, and sadly, does more harm than actual good. Researchers concluded that there is a history of an insecure attachment style, childhood neglect, and sexual abuse in individuals who cut themselves in many cases. Researchers also concluded that self-harm is gender-specific in the way it presents itself. Overall, more women were reported as involved in self-harm behaviors than men. In addition, women partook in more scratching, cutting, and damage to arms and legs. Even though some men were also reported to have inflicted self-harm, they were more in the form of burns and self-hitting, with most of the damage done to the face, chest, and genitals.

Over 75% of the people with BPD reported having made at least one attempt at suicide, with many trying multiple times in their lives. Suicidal BPD patients are also more likely to go through with suicide than other psychiatric disorders. Suicide is more common in BPD because it is a chronic condition, which leaves patients thinking about suicide daily for months or even years. These suicidal thoughts are further potentiated by increased impulsivity due to co-occurring alcoholism, severe emotional pain, and self-induced isolation, which hide signs of self-harm.

Symptom 6: Extreme Emotional Mood Swings

Another vital symptom experienced with BPD is extreme emotional mood swings. The shifting of a person's mood in a short period is the symptom that is most highlighted in popular media regarding BPD. One moment, the person might be on top of the world only to be followed by a low spirit and loss of hope mere moments later. The littlest of things uttered carelessly by someone could ruin their best moods and produce an extreme emotional response from within them.

Mood swings are a very regular human expression. They are expressed by almost everyone, regardless of whether they have a mental illness or not. However, in BPD, these mood swings are more pronounced in their intensity and last longer than regular emotional shifts. They are much more frequent too and occur from every few days to even a few hours.

You may have observed how a person with BPD might be feeling okay at one moment, but the next, they might be devastated, hopeless, and extremely sad for the most insignificant reasons. The extremity in mood swings often pushes people with BPD into an impulsive set of actions, consisting of anger outbursts, substance abuse, alcoholism, self-harm, and suicidal thinking to cope. A person with BPD experiences these shifts multiple times in a single day. This is different from an unaffected individual who does not suffer from this disorder; their mood swing episodes would typically occur once or twice during an entire week.

It is crucial to keep in mind that mood shifts also occur in Bipolar Disorder and can cause a misdiagnosis of Bipolar Disorder instead of BPD. The mood swings in Bipolar Disorder are usually more extreme, polarized, and accompanied by manic episodes. On the other hand, a person with BPD usually goes from anxious to angry or from depressed to edgy without reaching the extreme highs seen in someone with Bipolar Disorder.

Furthermore, there are some common associations of mood swings with BPD. Dissociation from oneself or not feeling in touch with one's observational reality, but feeling like an outsider in your tale instead is one of the major ones. Some people may also be susceptible to rejection, sense feelings of emptiness or paranoia, and be unable to make themselves feel better.

Mood swings, particularly those in BPD, are usually induced by external triggers. These shifts often occur in response to a perception of being abandoned, shunned, or rejected by another person. The fight or flight response is also more easily triggered in BPD. Turning off the brain's rational part and turning on the survival instincts contributes to mood swings. This attribute also leads to people starting fights with others for the smallest of reasons; even a harmless joke could be enough to trigger them. People with BPD are often seen to damage their relationships or friendships by constantly flipping out as the other person might not want to or does not know how to deal with their partner or friend's unpredictable emotional mood shifts.

Symptom 7: Chronic Feelings of Emptiness

As we move along further with the symptoms associated with BPD, you may have started to notice how each symptom is worse than the one before it. For example, the symptom we will be discussing in this point — a chronic feeling of emptiness — is one of the most important diagnostic criteria for BPD. The feeling of emptiness is a reflection of dysregulation of identity, and it can be devastating for many people suffering from BPD.

However, some people still do not understand what a feeling of emptiness exactly means. Emptiness presents itself as feelings of loneliness, but it is also complemented with extreme boredom, a lack of emotions, passion, and satisfaction in life. An individual with BPD may often feel nothing at all. A numbness envelops their being because they do not fully appreciate the purpose of their life. They are not content with their existence because they do not feel the drive to move forward, and their disconnection from life makes them apathetic to everything else. These feelings are often due to the exact reasons for all the other BPD symptoms listed so far; childhood trauma and controlling parents as they play a role in raising children who are indifferent to life's simple pleasures.

People experiencing emptiness often feel less motivated to stay productive. Things they had once enjoyed taking part in, such as art and music, eventually start to seem like a chore. They begin finding boredom in their hobbies. The culprits are the feelings of emptiness as they lead the individuals to fall behind on the drive they once had to excel in their careers, and they may stop trying to socialize, not even for work purposes. Teens and young adults might suddenly cancel their plans with friends and even refuse to attend classes and school events. They are also likely to stop working hard academically and get stuck in a vicious cycle of merely existing and not moving forward towards a greater purpose.

Most of these people often do not know why they feel this way, which adds to their increased guilt. This mental state pushes them further, making them feel even more disconnected from life. In addition to these emotions, not being content with who they are (i.e., identity disturbance) toppled with isolation can further hurt them as they begin to detach from every aspect of the outside world and aim towards a complete emotional numbing. All of this is partly due to hyperemotional sensitivity.

At first glance, it might be hard to believe that extreme emotional sensitivity in BPD can lead to emotional numbness. After all, the two terms seem to be quite the opposite. However, more often than not, emotional numbness is not a conscious decision, and many do not even realize what they are doing until it becomes a part of their routine. Instead, it may develop as a response to discovering that revealing their genuine emotions or intentions will lead to getting abandoned, rejected, or ridiculed. Thus, they decide that it is better to conceal their inner sensitivity to maintain social links and survive.

What starts as a pattern to hide from other people can lead to hiding from themselves and straight-up denying their own needs. This behavior is further induced in cases where the patient has experienced childhood neglect or repeated emotional traumas. This emotional detachment can be associated with long-term boredom, unwillingness, or, better yet, an inability to respond to certain events with happiness or joy. It is also hard for individuals to connect or build any intimate bond. And all of this to dampen their pain.

Chronic emptiness also has a strong tendency to lead to depression and hopelessness, which is why many suffering from it can have strong suicidal tendencies and are also more likely to self-mutilate. And thus, the cycle rejuvenates itself as self-harm, further isolating that individual from other people.

A lot of conversational signs of emptiness can present as comments such as, "I'm always lone," "no one cares about me," "I hate who I am," "I have no idea what to do with my life," or "I can never fit in with people." Along with this, many BPD patients are said to be in a detached protector mode where they are cut off from parts of their core self. Their comfort and safety needs are not being met, making them engage in impulsive behaviors, such as binge eating, drinking too much alcohol, or even cutting themselves without genuinely knowing why they are doing it. Some individuals may even have some memory loss due to living this robotic self-stimulating lifestyle, forgetting essential aspects of their past. They may look at an old photo of themselves, but when they see their old self, the photo may suddenly feel surreal to them. A case in point is a female patient convinced of not feeling any love for her spouse and attempted to end her marriage on an impulse.

Many BPD patients in therapy can enter this detached mode. During therapy, a person might be forced to question their behavior and become accountable, making them feel subconsciously threatened. <u>Therefore, their need to build up a wall to shield themselves becomes stronger.</u> They often fear the possibility of getting hurt again if they start feeling again after receiving treatment.

However, the problem that these individuals might face, despite numbing themselves to pain and negative emotions, lies in the feelings of frustration that will almost always eventually reach their limit. Sometimes, even minor events can, without any warning, cause these people to blow up and push them back into the need to deal with not only new emotions but with everything they had previously suppressed at an overwhelming force. And since they would have been numbing themselves to negative emotions for far too long, it may seem like these feelings of frustration have just recently shown up out of nowhere. This amplifies the pain even further.

Symptom 8: Explosive Anger

BPD patients often experience explosive anger. Its intensity level is so high that it is referred to as borderline rage, which is a very severe form of anger where individuals find it hard to function at baseline. The 5th Edition of the Diagnostic and Statistical Manual of Mental Disorders (DSM 5) describes BPD-specific anger as "inappropriate, intense anger that is difficult to control." It is described as inappropriate because it is too intense and extreme for the situation causing it. For example, the trigger could be a harmless joke or something utterly innocuous that others might not take offense to, but the reaction may be extreme. The anger usually takes the form of yelling, screaming, or sarcasm. It might even express itself in the form of physical violence that could even evolve into criminal behavior.

Borderline anger has been differentiated from regular anger. Recent studies have concluded that while the level of anger experienced by BPD patients is the same as that of ordinary individuals, the difference is in the duration of the responses. Anger subsides far more quickly over time for healthy individuals than in the case of people with BPD. Hence, the severity of anger in BPD patients refers not to the intensity but the duration of the anger. Borderline anger is further found to induce a person to obsess over their angry experience and thoughts repeatedly. This rumination occurs to the point that the person's repetitive thought cycle worsens their anger and increases its duration.

Borderline anger associated with BPD can distract individuals from focusing on their life goals, career, or any other important task. Therefore, this anger can lead to self-sabotage; the person under the influence of rage is more likely to internalize their perceived failures and rejections. Perceived rejection has a significant role in the genesis of borderline rage since BPD patients do not know how to deal with even the slightest hint of rejection from other people. This intense anger without any form of emotional regulation can lead an individual to become more aggressive or lash out to cope. Regrettably, most of these patients do not learn techniques to transmute or let the anger run its course, so the only outlet they are left with is a physical rage often targeted towards intimate partners.

This brings us back to outbursts of anger which are a common symptom of BPD. Most of the time, whenever BPD patients remember those who wronged them, angry emotions resurface again — no surprise there. Lashing out is partly in response to their idea of revenge, as they are less likely to forgive and move on from the past mistakes committed by the other person. The anger is also the only semblance of perceived control they might have over themselves, thereby proving that a person's rage is only a symptom of how little control they have over their life.

These episodes of anger and rage might also present themselves as self-mutilation in response to an argument or a long and angry rant about some person or instance. They are also expressed in more extreme and dangerous ways, such as physical assault on their children or spouse. Borderline rage can leave a person miserable; their relationships suffer, and sometimes, people even lose their lives. In addition, borderline rage is more likely to get a person to end up in trouble with the law.

However, people dealing with close ones suffering from BPD must realize that for that person, borderline rage is, in a way, their defense mechanism. Many end up with this rage due to continually bottling up their emotions in an effort to keep their guard up, so they do not drive people further away. They do not realize that a person cannot bottle up everything forever and a tipping point will eventually be reached. Therefore, borderline rage results from the dam breaking, where everything they had once bottled up comes crashing down. The neglected reality drowns the person in the wallows of their self-destructive rage. And since emotional dysregulation is a core element of BPD, most of these patients do not know how to deal with anger the way another person might.

Symptom 9: Feeling Suspicious/Out of Touch with Reality

As we are nearing the end of this chapter, we will discuss the last symptom of BPD, i.e., feelings of suspicion and being out of touch with reality. People with BPD are usually paranoid and suspicious about the motives of those around them, as you might have already guessed from the listed symptoms. However, this paranoia is often accompanied by losing the sense of what is real and what is not. These feelings lead to the brain experiencing a sense of fogginess that prevents them from perceiving the reality in front of them. The experience of losing a sense of reality is termed dissociation, which can almost be described as someone detaching from their own body.

The DSM 5 places paranoia as an essential diagnostic criterion for BPD as around 87% of the patients reported having experienced paranoia. This is usually induced by stress. Therefore, it is referred to as Paranoid Ideation, a phenomenon that also occurs in other disorders, such as Schizophrenia.

When someone experiences paranoia, they feel as if they are under severe threat all the time, as if other people are out to get them or are conspiring against them. It generally also transcends into a lack of trust for other people. Symptoms of suspicion and paranoia are varied; in some, they are more profound, while they may be milder in others. Paranoia can express itself as a general distrust of others, especially of a romantic partner's faithfulness. This leads to difficulties when forming healthy romantic relationships. However, these people do not only face problems in romantic relationships but all relationships in general. Paranoia can also be seen among people who feel like targets of perceived victimization. These people read the slightest body language signs among their social circles and perceive all social cues as hostile. They also often feel like the ones around them are stalking them. Of course, all of this is in their heads, but it leads to tremendous stress and increased social anxiety.

However, Paranoid Ideation should not be confused with Delusional Paranoia. The latter includes believing false information, usually for a fixed and consistent duration of time. Delusional beliefs have to persist for at least a month for a positive diagnosis for Delusional Paranoia. Whereas paranoia is shorter-lived, and the focus may keep changing in Paranoid Ideation, there is no consistency in belief. Moreover, unlike Delusional Paranoia, people with stress-induced Paranoid Ideation are not convinced of having concrete proof of their thoughts and conspiracies. In the case of Paranoid Ideation, paranoia symptoms are often relieved with the removal of stress, unless the source of stress is chronic and life endearing. In that case, paranoia relief might only be possible with medication or treatment.

Paranoia can also lead to losing touch with what is real and what is not, leading to what most people describe as Zoning Out. However, dissociation is still considered separate from paranoia, even if they are co-occurring. For example, have you ever observed someone with BPD and gotten the impression that he is constantly daydreaming? Or maybe they get invested in reading a book that they forget all about their surrounding environment? Or perhaps, they got into an accident because they forget to take a turn on the road? If yes, then it most likely that that person zoned out while doing their tasks.

Dissociation is a feeling accompanied by different

experiences, and depersonalization is one of them. It is the feeling of being separate from one's own body as if that person is observing their own body from the outside as a mere onlooker. It is like watching oneself in a dream. Depersonalization can manifest itself as robotic feelings and no control over speech or actions, an inability to personalize or own one's own memories, an inability to describe emotions, and the sense that one's limbs are distorted or swollen or shrunk. It often occurs alongside derealisation.

Derealisation is the feeling of detachment from the external world and its aspects, such as other people. What is otherwise familiar can appear new, strange, or surreal. The world as a whole may seem like a different dimension as if they are viewing it through a medium or a veil. It presents itself as a distortion of shapes, sizes, and distance in the real world and a sense of increased perception of your surroundings. It may even feel like recent events happened long ago. Visual blurriness and color distortion occur while shapes become two-dimensional or even downright cartoonish. In the case of depersonalization and derealisation, people are often aware that the visible changes are unreal. This can scare them and leave them further stressed out regarding their experiences.

Paranoia is also usually accompanied by amnesia, which is a form of memory loss with the inability to form new memories. People often zone out or lose all sense of time for minutes to even hours. Most of the time, they cannot even recall what they did while they were awake.

Identity confusion is the struggle of not knowing who one truly is. A person might base their individuality on someone else, like their spouse. This is already a very profound symptom of BPD. Identity alteration is when a person starts to act like someone else to the point that it is very evident to others, and they call the individual out on it. For instance, the person might perform a skill they do not recall ever learning. However, the persons suffering from identity alteration usually don't realize that they are acting like a different person.

The feeling of losing touch with reality or dissociation often occurs to those with abusive childhoods riddled with neglect. It is the brain's way of coping. Suppose you know someone who experienced a difficult childhood. In that case, the chances are that these attributes affected how they perceived themselves and used these to develop their personalities, carrying them onto their adult life.

CHAPTER 3
HELPING YOURSELF AND OTHERS

Dear reader, if you are still with us and invested in the book, we are grateful. We feel immense happiness knowing that you have stuck with us still and that we have not terrified you. However, there is plenty more that we would like to share with you! In the previous chapter, we discussed the nine major symptoms of BPD, a mental health issue with numerous unhealthy aspects. This chapter will now look at the positive aspects only; we threw enough information at you before to scare you for a lifetime.

When you think of mental health problems, what is the first thought that enters your mind? Whatever it may be, it's safe to assume that you probably do not label the person with the problems as "crazy." That is what has significantly changed over the years. In the past, there used to be a general stereotype associated with mental health issues; maybe some individuals believe in it still. Mental illnesses were allegedly the disease of the "insane," and anyone who was diagnosed with a mental illness was expected to be put in a psychiatric ward and punished with shock convulsions and all other sorts of retributions. That is what was primarily believed that these people deserved in the past. But we are happy to inform you that these thoughts and methods have slowly changed over the years as the world progressed.

In recent years, a lot of awareness has been raised on the issues regarding mental health. People are, bit by bit, opening up to the idea that mental health disorders are not wounds, as they were once believed to be; they do not imply that a person is crazy. Not everybody with problems in their mind needs to be shoved in a hole, hidden away from the whole world. The new thought process is also helping individuals open up to the idea of admitting to their mental health issues and seeking all the help they need.

That is what this chapter will be focusing on: helping yourself heal. BPD is a severe mental health issue with all of its grave negativities stuck to it. However, there is help available in all forms, and none of those include shock therapy. Phew! All mental illnesses can be helped if given a chance together with a positive outlook on life. And BPD is no different.

The words "crazy" and "insane" will not be mentioned moving forward. The use of these two words to describe any individual is not allowed, mental illness or not. We condone the usage of remarks that insinuate that a person may not be of sound mind. These words should not be used for anybody, including the people with BPD. We emphasize correct language usage because it plays an essential part in building or breaking a person's self-confidence. Using condescending language to describe people with mental health issues will further push them back into their shells, which is definitely not something you want to do. Think about this: How would you feel if you could not talk to your closest friend because they do not understand you?

If you are someone reading up on BPD because a loved one was recently diagnosed with it, this is the first thing that we would suggest for you to act upon. Using the right kind of language will significantly change the person you are dealing with. Being responsible with your words can help the person with BPD more than you think it will. It will make them believe that they are not as different from everybody else as they thought they were. They will begin to familiarize themselves with those around them and stop alienating themselves from the rest of the world as they used to. It will help build their confidence and assure them that people do not regard them differently or negatively. In turn, this change will help the persons with BPD to want to better themselves.

A human being cannot be forced to change themselves. Change in a person can only be brought about if that person wants. For example, consider kids. They are notorious for running around and causing havoc wherever they go. Kids do not act according to the situation, and they behave however they want. They are a ball of energy that is hard to calm down. However, it is not impossible to calm them down. If a child is running around at a formal event, but his mother grabs him firmly by the arm and uses a stern voice to order him to sit down in one place, what do you suppose is going to happen? The child might do as the mother says for some moments, but he will remain grumpy throughout the entire time and rebel. He will be even more challenging to deal with the next time they are out in public. He will deliberately act in a manner that would instigate his mother. On the other hand, if the mother had assumed a softer tone with her child and asked him to quiet down, calmly explaining to him how his behavior might seem disrespectful to others, there is a higher probability that he would have listened to her.

The same applies to people dealing with BPD. They simply want to be heard and understood. They want the people around them to treat them fairly. Therefore, individuals with BPD are more likely to get help if their situation is explained correctly without leaving anything out rather than merely forcing them into a rehabilitation center and expecting them to come out as new human beings. Force has never been a stimulating factor for change. Instead, it has always had the opposite effect on people, and rightfully so. Force has played a more significant part in regressing people backward rather than having them move forwards. People are not objects to be pushed around wherever and whenever you want. They are of flesh and blood like yourself, with their own feelings and emotions. Besides, it is highly disrespectful for somebody to have a stronghold on another person's life. You cannot be directing two lives in one lifetime. All individuals should be given the opportunity to make their choices for their life. You can help them in the process, but the final decision should always be theirs to make at the end of the day. Not yours.

The guide to helping a close friend or family is to be a good friend. People with BPD need the people they love to be there for them, to listen and understand them and the challenges they had to face in their past. Most of the time, their mental health worsens when the people in their lives do not understand their struggles or do not care enough to change their perspective as they might need to. BPD patients do not need others to call them out on their irrational behavior. Instead, it would be more beneficial to try to understand their point of view. Try not to tell them off. Instead, try to motivate them into doing things that will help them. Try to listen to them. Try to put yourself in their shoes. Once you do this, you will observe how simply good company can brighten up their lives and make them feel as if they are not alone in this world.

On another note, if you are reading up on BPD because you have been either diagnosed with it or think you have it, we want you first to clear your mind. Then, we want you to grab a pen and a piece of paper. Then resume reading and as you do so, start scribbling down the reasons you can think you are or can be diagnosed with BPD and how you can possibly help yourself. Do not take this in a negative light. Whether they have BPD or not, everybody should sit down and think to themselves about how they want to change at some point in their life. The change could be tiny, or it could completely modify your way of life. However, the point that we are trying to emphasize here is that you are not the only one. You are not alone. You are not the only person fighting their battles, and you sure will not be the last. You are not the only one with BPD, and you are not alone, even if, most days, you may think you are.

We want to start by complimenting you. It takes a tremendous amount of effort to admit to yourself that you need help. Then, it takes an even greater effort to try and receive that help with an open mind. If you are someone with BPD and started reading this book because you wanted to improve in any way possible, we want to say that we are immensely proud of you and your desire to do better. The desire to heal is always the first step towards change. It is also the most challenging step. It takes a lot of courage to be able to get up out of bed and say to yourself, "Today, I will try to be a better person."

What comes next is the motivation to maintain this mindset. From here onwards, you cannot choose the days you want to help yourself. You will need to be consistent and patient. Change does not come about in a day or a few days. It takes time to develop your new mannerism and make it a habit, but we assure you that it will all be worth it in the end when you come out as a better version of yourself.

A better version of yourself is precisely the end goal. When we say change, we do not mean that a person with BPD or any other mental illness needs to transform their identity or personality completely. What we mean is that individuals with BPD need to enhance the noble characteristics they possess and suppress the traits causing them hindrance in their relationships and work-life in any way. Deleting all bad attributes is a very romantic approach, but it is not the one that we are after for, sometimes, the somewhat dark qualities of a person can help them out in one way or another. Instead, our aim is for you to focus only on the positive aspects of your life. Start doing this as soon as you open your eyes in the morning. Be thankful for being able to get out of bed. You may not consider it a big deal, but it is a considerable achievement, and you should be proud of yourself for it!

Focus on the minor change at first. Go easy on yourself. Be kind to yourself. A pattern is noticed within people who seem to be stuck at one specific phase of their life for a long time; these people are hard on themselves. People who bring on self-pity and are only stuck on all things that go wrong in their life find it harder to move forward. The past prevents them from reaching a better future. Being stuck in the past will not let you enjoy your present, nor will it allow your future to prosper.

That is why we put a lot of emphasis on kindness. You need to be kind to yourself, and you owe yourself that much. Dealing with mental health every day of your life must be hard, including a disorder such as Borderline Personality. This grave issue can suck the fun out of a person's life. So if one day you wake up and feel demotivated to go about your day, that is okay. Everybody deserves a day off, and so do you. However, it is essential to realize when it's time to stop forcing yourself to function. We understand when you say that even the littlest of tasks, such as meeting friends, can drain you. So stop when your BPD gets overbearing. While positivity can be a good thing, toxic positivity can do you more harm than good. It would be a real shame if you moved a step backward after such amazing progress.

However, in all reality, you need to really look for the good positive things in life. Toxic positivity may be unhealthy, but an optimistic approach will help you move forward. After all, it has helped you want to pick up this book and help yourself. But you need to continue with this approach throughout your journey. There will be times when you will want to give up and spiral back down, but you cannot give in to that feeling. You will need to be strong till the end of the road. The road you are walking will have many obstacles that you will most likely have to face, but obstacles are a part of life. You cannot let them deter you from reaching your end goal. You will have to remind yourself why you want to bring a better change in your life every day. Repeat it over and over again like a mantra and instill it in your brain, so you never forget it.

This journey will be challenging, but life is all about facing hardships. If you could get things easily, would you really want them? Where would be the fun in that? The more you try, the harder it will get, and the fruitier the result will be. And in the end, when you have made it to your goal, accomplishing all that you wanted and beating your disorder, you will realize that all that waiting and struggle was worth it.

We wish you the best of luck on the journey ahead of you, and we hope you find happiness in it.

CHAPTER 4
POWER OF THE MIND

The brain is a very complex organ. In fact, it is the most complex organ of the body. It is the main head office that rules over the rest of the body. The body does what the brain commands it to do. Every action you perform, every word you speak is an order directed by the brain. But what if we were to tell you that it is really you, as an individual, that has all the power over the brain instead of the brain having complete control over you? It seems pretty contradictory to what we have been taught all our lives, right? But that is right, my friend. It is us who have all the control, all the power, over our brains. Not the other way around.

The brain is merely an organ. A vital one, no doubt. But it is simply a part of our body. It helps the rest of the body coordinate and performs its tasks successfully. That includes the heart, whose job is to constantly pump out blood into the rest of the body, digestion food in our stomach, and maintain a specific breathing rate at which we respire. All of these are significant involuntary functions of our body.

Pick out the keyword in the last sentence. The word "involuntary." What is so special about this? Our brains have mastered control over the body's involuntary actions, but it controls the voluntary actions only when we want them to. Do you see a difference here? Voluntary actions, such as the movements of our hands and feet, are under our control. The brain sure directs our limbs to move, but it gets that command from our subconscious. Let us suppose you are sitting at the moment and you want to get up out of your chair and move to the next room. Your brain will command your legs to help you get out of your sitting position and move your feet in the direction of the door. But your brain did not perform this action because it simply wanted to for the fun of it. And even if it wanted, it couldn't possibly happen. Your brain performed this act because your conscious mind wanted it to.

That is the key element we will be discussing in this chapter. If you have made it this far, do not stop now! We appreciate the progress you have made, and we congratulate you. But as we do so, we urge tar to bear with us a little longer. This chapter will be significant in helping you stay motivated throughout your journey of self-healing. We will be talking about how your mind is the most potent weapon you hold; it will either make or break your life. So we hope to convince you to use your mind in the best possible way you can to achieve the former.

The brain is merely an organ. The mind, however, is the real deal. That is where your subconscious resides. The mind is what gives you the ability to think. The mind is what helps you make correct or incorrect judgments. The mind is what gives birth to all the creative ideas you possess. It is where your memories reside. And the most important of them all is the mind, where your emotions and instincts are born. This last one is the one that relates most to BPD.

When we talk about mental health disorders, such as BPD, we indirectly imply that the problem is not reliant on the brain's structural aspect. Instead, the mind and the subconscious work in a slightly different manner than what society considers normal. We do not use the word "abnormal" because people's thoughts and emotions are moulded by their own personal experiences. We talked about how childhood trauma plays a massive part in BPD and that most of the symptoms are based on either childhood neglect or abuse. When these individuals with BSD were children growing up, they harbored their childhood memories and held on to the emotions and instincts born due to the circumstances they had to go through. So it is difficult to grow out of experiences that impacted the better part of a person's life — the years that build a person's character. This makes it is entirely understandable and definitely not abnormal for persons to behave in their own manner.

As you were reading this, one particular question must have come to mind: If these people's emotions are not abnormal, then why are they being diagnosed with mental health issues? The answer to that question is simple. There is a need for diagnosis if the feelings you are inhabited with begin impacting your life in a harmful manner. If your mood and your emotions are causing you to hurt yourself or delay your everyday routine for an extended period, mannerism needs to be given a name. It is not done to make the person feel like they are different from others regarding their mental capacity; mental illnesses are named more to help the doctors recognize them while enabling them to tread the various aspects of a condition with ease.

However, is the mind really affected by an illness, as people like to put it, or a person's past? A person's history contributes a great deal to the building process of their personality. The past merely consists of a chain of events, but a person's reaction to events influences their mental state. Most mental health problems all over the globe are were mainly caused by some form of traumatic experience in their past. They all have this one thing in common; somebody's words or actions elicited some form of a reaction, leading them to become the persons they are today.

The brain is like a record; it has all of the previous memories jotted down and stored inside it. When a person is still a child, they most often do not understand their situations. But all those instances are recorded and stored in the mind of the young child. As they grow older, they start to make sense of whatever they had seen growing up and begin forming opinions and developing emotions related to those past events.

Do you notice something odd here that might contradict your beliefs? The situations children are put in do not cause them any pain or hurt at that moment in time. However, as the years pass and they grow into adults, they try to recall those memories. As they do so, they try to understand what had been going on back then and express what they might think are the appropriate emotions for those events. So it is not the events themselves to be blamed but that person's psychological response to a particular event. This eventually starts to give rise to what is now referred to as mental health problems.

Every human has a brain that works differently from another person's. All humans have their own experiences that they have lived through, and so all humans will react differently. However, even when two people go through a particular event together, each individual has a different response to the event. While one person may have come out with minimal trauma, another could be distinctly disheveled by the circumstances. For example, let us take the most common cause of mental illnesses: an abusive childhood. Suppose the father verbally and physically abused two siblings who lived in the same house growing up. This type of case would cause obvious trauma. However, there still could be a very significant difference between the two siblings. One of them may grow up with relatively lesser problems. Maybe, that child develops relatively mild anxiety and depression because of his or her past. But the other sibling might have been more affected, developing a severe mental illness, such as Post-Traumatic Stress Disorder. Now, both of these siblings had gone through the same experiences, but they grew up to be different people with distinct personalities and a diverse set of problems. This example goes to show that every individual's thought process is different from anyone else's. Every individual expresses various emotions and forms different opinions about their situations, even if they are the same.

This example brings us to how an emotional reaction can form an individual's whole personality. A lot of the time, people find it easy to let their emotions control them. They let their feelings dictate their mood and actions. For instance, suppose a person was hurt by something their friend said to them. They thought what their friend told them was highly insensitive and let that thought process control them. This person was angry for the entirety of the day because of that one particular event, allowing that to become their mood for the day. Now, suppose the person goes to bed and wakes up the next day in the same spirit. And then they wake up the next day with the same mood, then the next, then the next over and over again. The cycle continues until people start to recognize the individual's angry and bitter reaction to everything over the weeks. His bitter temperament now identifies this person. After months of the same type of behavior, this particular individual assumes this temperament as one of his personality traits. Therefore, that individual allowed his emotions to guide him into a painful future. It is this person's reaction that paved the way for a troubled future. Instead of taking another's comment negatively, they could have simply ignored it and moved on with their life. That would have saved them the distress. Except, it is easier said than done.

Controlling one's mind and emotions seems like an arduous task. Past actions have an enormous influence on a person's mind, which could dictate their future. However, if one lets their past emotions dictate their future, the future will not be much different from the past. Suppose memories are continuously hovering over a person's mind, reminding them of every negativity that had once affected them. In that case, it will stop that person from moving forward. Instead, they keep reliving their past every moment of their present life; their memories have a hold on every phase of their life. Because of the repetitive actions, thoughts, and emotions that a person limited themselves to, their body starts to believe it's living in the same experience. They form an unhealthy routine that the body begins to follow subconsciously. The pattern to which they adapt makes them behave like a program, where the person himself is the computer. The same way a computer works by following a specific program, the person starts to follow their routine subconsciously, without realizing whether they need to update it or not. The person does not even realize their pessimistic approach to life until they have already adopted it into their lifestyle.

This way of living has been scientifically proven to be unhealthy for the body. Your body has certain stress hormones, most dominantly the Cortisol hormone. In stressful situations, the body releases a set of hormones that bring about physiological changes in response to a perceived threat. The response system that the body portrays in these situations is known as the "Fight or Flight" response. It is an active defense reaction of the body that gives the person the strength to either fight and deal with the situation head-on, or flee the situation as fast as possible, thus the name. This response is a relatively short; the body gets an adrenaline rush that helps them fight or escape the situation, and then the rush settles down. However, these hormones could have nasty long-term effects on the body. The hormones for stress down-regulated genes and can even create a disease that could make us sick. So what do you understand by this? By stressing ourselves out and expecting the worst from every person and every situation, we humans make ourselves physically sick. So then, if the brain is actually capable of bringing us a disease, shouldn't it be able to bring us health as well?

The mind works in mysterious ways, but man has found ways to reign some control over it. A large majority of the mind is your subconscious; people work in ways they have accustomed themselves to over the years. However, approximately 5% of your brain is still under your control. You can convince it to do anything. Whatever beliefs you hold on to will eventually become your reality. It is what you hold predominantly in your mind that makes its way into your life. You attract what you believe in. So while your subconscious mind, with all of its stored memories, has a more prominent role to play, it is you who is in major control of your future.

For those who are unaware of the placebo effect, it is a fake treatment provided to patients. That seems pretty unnecessary, right? Then why go through all the trouble of giving a person a false drug? The placebo drugs were used in experiments to check the effectiveness of the authentic drugs during clinical trials. They are inactive tablets or medical treatment given to one group of people, while others receive the original treatment. An interesting conclusion was drawn from these experiments. Both groups of people, both the ones taking the actual medication and the ones taking the placebo medication, exhibited beneficial effects. Around one-third of the people who were given placebo pills felt better without receiving an existing treatment for their problems. So all of this only reaffirms further the mind controls everything.

The interesting thing was that the people receiving the placebo pills were not told that they were not given the correct medication. On the contrary, they believed they were being given the proper treatment to cure whatever condition they were suffering from. But, in reality, they were given either sugar pills or multivitamins that would not affect their condition. When these pills are administered to the patients, most of the patients started feeling better. Whatever problem they had been going through seemed to improve itself. The placebo effect was discovered then, owing to the betterment of the crowd's issues.

You may be wondering how it is possible to achieve results

without receiving proper treatment. The deal here is primarily the individual's state of mind. It is not that people do not have any illnesses or were misdiagnosed with one. Instead, people with pathological conditions might start feeling better if they adopt a positive attitude towards their disease and its treatment.

People who were given the placebo pill thought they would begin to feel better because they had received the treatment. In their mind, they trusted the professionals and their ability to make them better. So, with an optimistic approach to treatment, their mind started to make the body believe that the medication was working. In reality, the drug was not even administered. However, the mind's ability to make the body act the way it wants it to is so strong that it ultimately succeeded in making these individuals feel better.

Just like there are opposites of all words and phenomena in life, the placebo effect also has a counterpart. The nocebo effect has the exact opposite effect. While the placebo works positively in favor of an inactive treatment, the nocebo effect negatively results in the same fake treatment. Similar experiments to the ones showing the placebo effect were conducted by giving a phony medication to a group of people. Even though the sugar pills or multivitamins did not have side effects, some people manifested so much negativity into their life that they began to experience adverse effects instead of getting better.

Suppose a person with an illness goes to the doctor. This patient is receiving the best treatment with a high probability of the disease being cured. However, despite all the odds being in their favor, their condition starts to worsen. Most times, this outcome is a result of their negative mindset. It is the result of the expectation of a negative outcome, despite there not being a chance of one, attracting the sickness to them. That is the strength of your beliefs.

Your beliefs guide you to either your success or your downfall. And in this way, your belief system forms a part of your personality and predicts your future.

What does that tell you about your mind? Your mind can do whatever you want it to. It can give you the results that you desire. What you think is what you get. That is how influential your thoughts are. Your mind will be convinced of whatever you want it to believe. It is how it worked with placebo and nocebo treatments; the patients' minds thought what they wanted it to believe. As a result, their minds worked to either improve their body's condition or to worsen it.

Similarly, if a person were to believe in a specific state of living, their minds would attract it into their lives. You can convince your mind to do anything you want. You are the one who holds all the power. So the next time you think of the impossible, remember that nothing is impossible. You only need to start believing in yourself.

The mind may be superior in its ability to lead one's life. However, it is, after all, equivalent to a machine. It cannot tell fiction and reality apart. This sounds rather bizarre, do you not think so? When we say fiction, we are not talking about unicorns and dragons; we mean dreams and nightmares. When a person experiences a terrible nightmare, they wake up panting and gasping for air, their heart racing as if they were dealing with the situation first hand. It is the mind that perceived this experience as a reality and made the body react accordingly. The mind deals with all problems the way it has been trained to by the individual. Hence, it does not decipher between actual instances and instances made up while unconscious. According to this theory, our thoughts and attitude form our habitual behavior.

For people with mental health disorders, including BPD, this is fantastic news. Your brain can change and work however you want it to. You may be going through a real tough time at the moment, but you have to stay positive in times like this! You have to attract a constructive change in your life through a set of firm and confident beliefs in your ability to do better. Life may seem hard right now, but things will eventually get better as you ingrain optimism in your mind. We want you to know that you can do it. People have done it in the past, and people are doing it right now.

Think of the person that you want to become. Think of the happiness that will envelop you once you reach your goal and let it motivate you the entire way. With the help of this book, a positive outlook, and professional help, you will, too, be happy in your relationships with others and with yourself.

CHAPTER 5
STABILITY

Thanks for still staying with us! This is going to be an exciting chapter as it is all about action and execution. You will probably return to this chapter many times to implement proper change. In the previous chapters, we talked about how one's mind and subconscious play a massive part in recovering and dealing with BPD. In this chapter, we shall now discuss how you can go beyond your mindset and implement a plan of action if you have committed yourself to this worthwhile road with the aim of freeing yourself from BPD and coming back out as a better person entirely.

The subconscious is your weapon, and you are the one with the power to execute your plans and use this weapon to the best of your advantage. The bedrock of your core subconscious self is the culmination of every habit you may have as of now. Therefore, building consistent and productive habits will be vital in constructing a sense of stability in your life. The highs and lows of BPD are already too hard to navigate through and have probably caused you enough worry as it is. Hence we need to help you move to a more balanced road. Keeping an equilibrium is always better than walking at the extremes.

Stability here refers to your ability to respond to the events around you with proper coping mechanisms. It refers to a consistent routine to occupy your idle hours and the will to endure all the problems that life will keep throwing your way. This is something you will get better at once you commit to this goal with absolute conviction. You owe it to your future self to stay with us and use this chapter as a blueprint to success!

But before delving into all the details on how you can achieve a stable and consistent routine, we shall first look at why they are essential in the first place. That way, we hope you will get all the motivation you need. The values and opinions of people with BPD are constantly fluctuating. Sometimes, they even oppose each other. It is almost as if they possess no valid fundamental beliefs in the first place. That insinuates that they cannot stand ground for something they genuinely believe in or something they believe is correct. This phenomenon, which makes it seem like these people are easily susceptible, will make them look less authentic. But human beings value the authenticity of other individuals a lot. It is the very defining quality that good leaders, good friends, and healthy romantic partners possess. Therefore, since people with BPD appear to lack these qualities, it makes it very hard for other people to rely on them, consequently damaging their social interactions. This can impede one's career in any business or professional environment as it will be hard to get along with other coworkers. Apart from that, it can severely impact one's performance when it comes to assignments, jobs, or any creative endeavors that need to be completed.

A consistent routine is essential in everyone's day-to-day life for emotional regulation and to give life a proper sense of meaning or purpose. Without a stable routine, it can be hard to get pretty much anything of importance done. No routine means no work is being done, and doing no work will only make a person feel worse than they already do. Human beings are not meant to function without aspiring towards a more significant goal. We all have things we want to achieve and claim, and having a planned and stable routine will do that for us.

Apart from these features, an essential tie-in to stability is coping healthily. One needs to replace toxic coping mechanisms, such as self-mutilation, binge eating, drinking too much alcohol, or any other harmful behaviors with healthy ones. That will allow a person to function through the stress of BPD and, after some practice, make them more confident in their ability to manage their emotional dysregulation. Most coping mechanisms discussed in this chapter are pretty straightforward to actualize, so do not stop reading just yet!

This is important because we do not want you to be further stressed out. We want you to feel better using simple methods. For instance, anytime you feel stressed, anxious, or sad, you can try listening to music that invokes positivity, hope, or excitement. Music is a great tool to make you momentarily feel better and, at the same time, can serve as an excellent means of distraction from negative thoughts. There are a plethora of YouTube channels online that have playlists that cater to specific styles and purposes. For example, you might find music mixes for relaxing, for focusing, or even to feel more driven and motivated. Merely concentrating on the meaningful lyrics of a motivational song can make a person want to improve themselves or finish a task on the get-go.

You could even dance it out to your favorite hits. That brings us to another coping method, called "Behavioral Activation," where a person participates in a non-passive, active activity. That includes activities such as dancing, taking a short walk, taking a cold shower, playing an outdoor sport for a while, or even cleaning your room. The activity has to be something that can distract you for a more extended amount of time while also yielding certain benefits. For instance, cleaning your room is an excellent example of how a person with BPD can immerse themselves in a healthy activity. This particular activity will not just limit fixing the external environment but also help you manage your sense of being by doing something that is entirely under your control. Therefore, cleaning your room can act as a small therapeutic jump before you dive into fixing more significant aspects of your life.

However, sometimes you might not feel like getting up at all, or you are feeling completely exhausted. On these occasions, it might be a good idea for you to ride out the wave of discomfort. It may seem hard at first, but it is worthy to note that the urge of impulsivity or the need to indulge in harmful escapist activities only remains high for a few minutes, after which it subsides.

Therefore, you must learn to recognize when these emotions or urges are arising and accept them as a part of yourself. Reacting with fear will only leave you more ill-prepared in dealing with such thoughts. Instead, accept your internal strife and tell yourself that it is okay to feel like this. These thoughts do not define you, and you do not have to act upon them. Then, focus on breathing deeply and exhaling. Notice every breath, every movement, everything around you, and everything you are currently feeling. This practice is known as "Being Mindful" since it basically encompasses being aware of oneself and one's place within the external realm. Doing so will allow you to cruise through the demanding impulses. At first, this might be slightly difficult but do not give up. We promise you that with some practice, you will get better at riding these waves out. Ultimately, mindfulness will also contribute to a better and more disciplined version of yourself.

This very same mechanism is tied into meditation, another technique you can try to calm and ground yourself. You could even whisper and tell yourself that you are safe, that you are okay, that nothing will harm you, and that despite whatever is internally haunting you, you will get through it and persevere. You will come out of it even stronger.

You could even try your hand at spirituality or religion. Different people may have different sorts of bonds with their religious affiliations. It may help if you prayed or at least welcomed the idea that an extraordinary being is watching over you, that you are not alone, that you are understood somewhere in the dimension of divinity. You might even find yourself calmer after praying or visiting a holy place of worship, depending on your religious affiliations.

A spiritual mindset may help a person break the shackles of seeking validation from others and their opinions. It may also solidify a person's internal faith that there is more to life than sensory stimuli. Research has proven how religion and spirituality can help people in dealing with internal stress. A person's religious devotion can often lead to decreased reactivity from external pressures. Even when the people around you may seem to be against you, your connection to God or a being of a higher power may give you the faith and resilience to carry yourself forward. A religious setting can even unite you with members of the same religion. For instance, attending a church congregation or Friday prayers at the mosque might possibly allow you to feel safer within the larger brotherhood of faith. These practices can help counter any feelings of loneliness or isolation as you will share a crucial and fundamental aspect of yourself with several other individuals.

This brings us to the importance of people and adequate healthy socialization. You need good people surrounding you, good people who care for you, and understand how BPD should not be a factor driving the two of you apart. People with BPD often miss hangouts with friends, possibly causing an increasing rift between the person with BPD and the rest of the group. But the best relationship-building between two individuals will occur when there is an effort from both parties. Thus, close friends or family members must have the proper knowledge regarding BPD, specifically when it comes to caring for someone who has this mental disorder. They should be there to help these people navigate through symptoms and counter their anti-social behavior.

At the same time, people with BPD are required to make an effort as well to mend any dynamic with a friend or romantic partner. For this reason, it is always recommended that you share your recovery journey with someone you can trust, and more importantly, someone you can rely on. You do not have to be alone in this, and having someone watching your back will make the entire process more smooth. Having someone walk this journey by your side will keep you more accountable to deliver on your promises to yourself and your loved ones. You will also be able to share your feelings, struggles, and thoughts with that someone, someone who will probably understand you. Their ongoing support and comfort can be reassuring for you during the course of your management. A close one might even remind you of any critical medication that you must take since they will try to help you along the way, constantly reminding you of what you must do to get better, even when you are at your lowest. In case of any setbacks, you will have a shoulder to rely on, making it less likely for you to further spiral into destructive coping mechanisms, such as self-harm or binge eating. A good friend, family member, or an understanding partner can push you into staying consistent with your therapeutic goals on this arduous journey.

That being said, you should try not to drive them further away. It may be hard, even for a trusted partner, to completely understand your struggle. That is a regular occurrence as BPD awareness is generally low among the general population. But you can help them familiarize themselves with your state better and therefore help them in assisting you. That way, not only will your own recovery be guaranteed, but your relationship can reach a greater height of mutual understanding as well.

An essential aspect of coping needs to be the way you navigate through the eventual triggers you may face at some point or another in life. Most patients dealing with BPD have specific triggers that may exacerbate their symptoms and make their day-to-day life even more difficult. Reactions to stimuli can include extreme impulsive outbursts of action, fear, tension, or sudden urges for self-harm. The best and most obvious way to deal with your triggers is to avoid them downright altogether.

To do this, you first need to identify what your triggers are, as they can vary from person to person. However, you might already have an idea of the general things that may trigger your impulsive outbursts from past experiences. But to do this properly, grab a pen and a notebook and sit in a quiet room with as little outdoor distraction as possible. Of course, you must be in a relatively stable mood before doing this since you will have to assess and think about your triggers. Divide the page into three columns. The heading of the first column will be "trigger," that of the second one will be "emotion," and the third column will be labeled "response to emotion." The next step is to recall the times you have ever experienced extreme adverse reactions such as impulsivity, anger, sadness, or fear. You can even note down any external event that may have occurred around you, like getting into an intense argument with a spouse or something anyone mentioned or said to you. Then try to fill out the column for emotions. If you struggle with categorizing complex feelings, you may choose from one of the six basic emotions: happiness, sadness, fear, disgust, anger, and surprise. You may even find it better to combine two or more emotions to understand better the complexity of what you must have felt in response to the trigger. Now, for the response column, write down how you reacted to that specific feeling. Make sure that you do not judge yourself too harshly while you recall your response. In fact, please, do not judge yourself at all! You are doing this to avoid repeating these sets of behaviors in the future.

You may have even responded to an emotion in a positive manner that did not involve any self-harm or impulsivity. If you did, make a note of that positive response. You need to remember the tactic you use then and put it to practice more often. Otherwise, just take a note of it, and repeat the previously mentioned steps for more triggers and their respective emotions and responses. In essence, you are listing down your triggers and what they basically lead to. Once you think you have listed down enough triggers, you should carefully analyze them and see how they all fit together in the bigger picture.

You will probably notice some pattern regarding the types of events that led to each trigger episode. For example, you might notice a sense of rejection or fear of abandonment as recurring triggers and emotions. Similarly, you might realize that you might have a peculiar way of coping in response to the emotions, such as by inflicting self-harm, reacting angrily, or binge eating junk food. The points that repeat themselves are going to be the most important ones.

This list will be used in the future to help you log your feelings. Keep noting your triggers all the way up to their respective responses, and eventually, you should be able to start predicting how you will act in response to those particular events or circumstances. This is going to be empowering for you because now, you will be able to avoid these triggers in the first place. For example, you might notice how you are more likely to engage in overconsumption of drugs or alcohol when in the company of a specific individual. In that case, that person can be a trigger for you. Or you could notice that looking at pictures of your ex-husband or wife can trigger you, which means that the best solution to overcome this might be to avoid looking at their photographs or blocking them on social media altogether.

That being said, we wish it were that simple. If only it could be as easy as avoiding every source of our worries and stresses. We completely understand that you might not be able to completely cut all triggers out of your life that easily, which brings us to the fact that a lot of triggers cannot and should not be avoided. For instance, if your boss at work is a trigger for you, then you cannot avoid them; they are the ones who will be giving you your paycheck at the end of the month. Avoiding every trigger can prevent you from dealing with issues at work or home, limiting your life to only comfort and leaving very little room for you to grow into a developed and mature individual.

This avoidance tactic should be used simultaneously with learning how to face your triggers in the long run. This method involves you facing many triggers at the same time, which might be mentally overwhelming at first. You may even consider taking a more gradual approach to this by asking for the help of a therapist.

Don't try to face all your triggers at once. Instead, start by selecting a single trigger, one that may be smaller than the others or not as severe in its responses. Then devise a plan on how you will tackle it and intentionally try facing the trigger. For example, if scrolling through an ex's Instagram triggers you, you can deliberately expose yourself to this trigger. Only this time, you will try to react in a different way than you usually do. For example, instead of responding with anger or impulsivity, you should try to meditate or do a set of 20 push-ups. This is to convince yourself that you can face discomfort and negative emotions without having to rely on the destructiveness of something as harmful as self-mutilation. If you keep practicing this, you will eventually develop a healthy habit of coping with one of your triggers. This is what we call progress!

To tackle the severe triggers that shake you to the core might not be as easy, but it is not impossible. Start by making a list of the multiple ways you can act to manage the trigger episode so that anytime the trigger event arises again, you can use the list to carry out your coping activities one after the other one. The good thing about this strategy is that there is no "one method." You will have the flexibility to try out different coping mechanisms. In trying them out, you will essentially ride out the urge to react negatively or successfully deal with the trigger itself. Apart from these methods, it is a good idea to talk to your therapist about everything you may have experienced to get further professional help or support.

We also need to talk about the power of the pen when it comes to coping with your demons. It has been reported that expressive writing and journaling have a positive effect on those dealing with BPD. As the name suggests, expressive writing consists of writing about anything you might want to, ranging from personal experiences, your persistent feelings, and responses to understand yourself. Your written records can remain private; simply writing about them will allow you to manage your internal thoughts. You can even turn this into a creative venture, such as poetry or even writing your own book. There is a lot of room for opportunity in online blog writing as well. This will also connect you with new people and land you a place in a lucrative platform where you can share everything that you feel. Writing can also serve as another cost-effective hobby that you can partake in whenever you feel unstable. Try to imagine unloading all the pressure and toxicity from within as your pen jots traces every line of ink. You can even scribble and draw alongside your notes, transmuting your inner turmoil into a written or artistic work that may allow other people to understand and, maybe, even admire you.

Another thing to consider would be bullet journaling. This

is basically a combination of a personal diary, daily planner, and to-do list, which will be used to record the past, organize the present, and plan the future according to its designer Ryder Carroll. The journal can record achievements, aspirations, and thoughts. You can even use it to commit to a specific goal and track your progress towards achieving it on a daily to weekly basis. Having recorded evidence of your progress will keep you more accountable and motivated, helping you refrain from giving up. Anytime you may feel like giving up, looking back at your journal can re-orient you back on your goal.

The journal's system consists of a future log to list down your goals, a monthly calendar to track short-term tasks or deadlines, and a daily record for managing the present, immediate deadlines, and daily tasks. There is also an index at the beginning to help you organize everything, track what is in the journal, and where to find it. The journal also uses different symbols for better organization and lets you see what you have planned for the days ahead. For example, events may be marked with a circle, while a dash would draw tasks on the to-do list. Such a system can seem arduous at first, but it will save time in the long run. You can use this one system instead of separately using calendars, planners, or applications. The symbols used will help in visually reminding you of your different goals. The journaling itself will help curb emotional dysregulation as it will aid you in getting out your thoughts.

While the structure and thought that goes into a bullet journal can be suitable for those who like staying organized, it can be slightly daunting or tiresome for someone to put up with all its complexity. Users who want a more straightforward approach can opt to personalize their bullet journals. They only focus on a few tasks or aspirations at a time and avoid the stress associated with too much-cluttered information. Keep in mind that the end goal here is to help you in your journey, so do what is the most convenient for you!

We hope that this chapter helped you. There is still a long way to go, but be sure to remember that we, along with all of your loved ones, are right here beside you. Just as you can go to your friends and family whenever you have your lows, you can pick up this book to read. Helpfully, this will remind you that you are not alone in your journey.

We wish you the best of luck!

CHAPTER 6
CREATING AN IDENTITY

As you are well aware by now, disturbances or inconsistency in one's identity can negatively steer them away from character-defining goals, beliefs, values, and actions. Previously, we talked about healthy coping mechanisms that can help with immediate urges. We also established the importance of shifting from a guilt-based outlook to a more forgiving mindset regarding oneself.

The next step will help you find yourself or rediscover who you truly are in more precise terms, which is precisely the topic of this chapter. This step to rediscovering yourself is an important one as the journey to crafting the new you cannot exist without having a blueprint of what you aspire to be. Every project needs a vision of what its end form is supposed to look like. In this particular case, the blueprint is your inner self and identity. That is the thing that gives you meaning and purpose in life.

The first step that we recommend is to find a good

therapist. Therapy is hyper-personalized, and a therapist can get to know you very well, thereby allowing them to provide you with the best reliability, advice, and communication, which induces accountability. However, before diving into the different types of programs and therapies available out there, we will first talk about what you can do right now to kickstart the search for who you are. The only way one can live with purpose instead of just letting life carry them from one place to another is by identifying what you truly want and value in your existence.

A person's inner persona is the sum of their core values. It can be anything that might have motivated you at some point in life, anything that might have inspired you to think about this world deeply. It can be anything that resonated deep within you. An idea, an abstract, a phenomenon, a trait, or even someone that reflects a set of values you genuinely admire as a source of inspiration. Anything that you want to acquire as part of your inner being.

Core values are unique from one person to another as everyone goes through a different set of events that shape what they consider meaningful. That being said, some crucial ideals that aspire the majority of us to live by include physical well-being, meaningful and honest friendships, healthy relationships, prospering careers, or responsible community contribution.

Make a list of values that you are sure you embody within yourself, not the ones you might wish you possessed. Even though it is good to acquire the positive traits you wish you had, it is essential to first recognize your core values. The one you already own. Identifying them will help you find your inner motivators, the source of your drive.

After you are done listing these values, it is time to rate

them, depending on their importance to you. For instance, allocate 0 points for the values of no importance, 1 point for the values with some importance, and 2 points for your top priority values. This step requires deep introspection. Now, think about whether you are prioritizing your given values in life. Ask yourself whether you are living your life based on these values, if you are following them and using them to guide your actions or not. If your values do not align with your actions, that means you are not satisfied with life. Only when the two align can you live in the moment with inner peace.

To obtain more clarity over your perceived values, try writing a statement or the desired goal in front of a value that you consider important. For example, if health and fitness are one of your core values, write, "I want to reach 75 kg and below 10% body fat percentage by lifting weights and getting help from a trainer." For your career, you could wish for something like, "I want to excel in making enough money to support my disabled parent." These intention statements may help to remind you why the values you listed are so important in your eyes, revealing your true intentions. To be completely honest with yourself here, we all have different convictions that bind us to a particular ideal or core value.

Despite the importance of values, they are not the only pillar of one's identity. One's purpose is something equally important but harder to determine. An individual's purpose is an integral part of how they identify themselves. Having a solid purpose has been closely linked to making more money, working harder, improved sleep, reduced risk of heart attack, and reduced likelihood of depression. Hence, we shall discuss several ways how you can find your purpose.

It is always a good idea to open up to the insight of those

around you. They may offer feedback on topics that you consider purposeful. Other people may be unbiased and possibly see you differently than how you view yourself. Think of how they compliment you. Or better yet, ask someone what they think your passion or great trait is. It could be something like competitiveness or quirky like a great sense of humor. Their answers can reinforce your road to finding yourself.

This method proves helpful with a healthy group of friends. However, you need to surround yourself with such individuals anyway if you want to pursue your passions. The last thing one needs is the company of people that drag them down into a spiral of negativity. You have a better chance of finding your purpose if you are surrounded by individuals trying to do the same to grow themselves. Negative friend or family circles can thrive on your self-esteem issues, using it in their favor to do their bidding or take advantage of you. Better people will help you grow beyond these issues by inspiring you to follow your passions with conviction. Therefore, a healthy group of friends and family can teach a lot and motivate you enough to follow your core values.

One of the best things you can start doing to find meaning in life and ultimately create an identity is to pursue helping other people. By being a giver or a helper in somebody else's life, you will find more meaning behind your existence. Knowing that someone is doing better because of you and the help you gave him is one of the most gratifying feelings contributing to your self-worth. We are not asking you to start volunteering or donating to charity. No, what we are asking of you is much simpler. You could help your neighbor or anyone else by merely lending a hand for a minor task. By helping other people, you will open up social connections, learn to forgive yourself more, and realize that everyone needs help. There is no shame in letting someone help you. Give and take is one of the most primal forms of transaction.

You could even try your hand at new activities like swimming, joining a new club, creating a blog, or signing up to learn a new skill. Such actions can pave the road to crafting the latest version of who you will be.

Apart from finding meaning or purpose, it is equally important to consider specific treatments to work through identity disturbances suffered from in BPD and counter the emerging self-image issues. Most of the programs we will mention are strongly tied to therapy. Therefore, for the majority of them, you will have to first reach out to a therapist.

Cognitive Behavioral Therapy (CBT) is centered around identifying self-limiting, anxiety-inducing thoughts or beliefs that may prevent you from pursuing your life goals. The steps usually involve identifying the problem you might be dealing with, listing down the possible solutions, and analyzing the pros and cons of each solution. This will help you identify the best one, after which you move on to its implementation. These steps, along with self-monitoring and accountability from a therapist, can significantly help with negative identity traits such as addiction, anger, impulsivity, and escapist tendencies. In addition, CBT will change your thinking process, thereby allowing you to build a new set of beliefs. As we all know by now, your beliefs and inner convictions shape your true self.

Your therapist might even recommend Dialectical Behavioral Therapy (DBT) which can teach you to live in the moment. This form of therapy involves using mindfulness practices to disassociate yourself from any harmful beliefs or behaviors. This therapy assumes various forms, ranging from individual therapy to group therapy sessions, where you are taught new personality-building skills with other individuals. In addition, you will be taught "Distress Tolerance," which consists of building the resilience to deal with any form of discomfort or distress in a healthy way. Again, this is important in defining the person you are going to be in the future.

Apart from these, many other therapeutic programs can be very beneficial. For instance, "Transference Focused Psychotherapy" can help approach your feelings and relationships, which also contributes to constructing your inner self to a great degree.

By combining therapy with the various ways of finding your purpose mentioned above, together with things you can do to make your life more meaningful, you will notice a stark difference in your sense of self. As a result, the opinion you hold of yourself will change for the better, and that shall open various doors for the new you!

CHAPTER 7
EXTREMES OF BPD

BPD in itself is a severe mental health disorder, as we have seen thus far. It manifests itself in various forms among different individuals who suffer from the disorder. While some people may exhibit mild symptoms, there is a slight majority who eventually lose control over their minds. BPD can turn very ugly very quickly, and we do not want that to happen. This chapter deals with the extremities of BPD that could eventually lead to a BPD crisis.

A BPD crisis could end up being life-threatening for the individuals dealing with the disorder. Why? These crisis periods lead to the illness taking up complete control over the individual's mind. With mental health issues, including BPD, patients often report having felt as if all power had been snatched away from them. In these cases, when a crisis occurs, individuals succumb to their anger or their depression, letting their intense emotions be the leader of their actions. It is as if the individual's subconscious has been warded off to the very back of the mind. Instead, the parts of the mind hazed by the emotions are granted total control and allowed to rule over this disorder. Thus, the extreme emotions of either mania or depression associated with BPD dominate, dictating the brains of the people it affects.

Now imagine losing control like this. If you are a reader who is not suffering from this disorder, this explanation is the closest you will ever get to understand how your friends or family members with BPD feel. Try to put yourselves in these shoes. You cannot even imagine living your life being dictated by an illness, can you? It is difficult, but we can make it better. As we move deeper into the extreme emotions people with BPD experience, we will do our utmost to help you understand better what they really have to go through. If, however, you are a reader with BPD, hang in there. This chapter will also be covering specific ways how you can gain back control over your mind. You are your ruler. You can overthrow the illness if you only believe that you can.

Now, we come onto the more intense symptoms of BPD. Can you guess which ones need to be more delicately handled? It turns out that even though all the nine major symptoms are very hard to deal with, the most extremely challenging ones for people with BPD to control are anger issues and self-harming behavior.

Managing one's anger is an arduous task as the raging feelings haze one's mind, taking all the control for itself and leaving the person entirely at its mercy. Anger is an emotion that many people with and without BPD have a hard time controlling. So for those of you with anger management issues, the self-help tricks in this chapter might be of use to you too!

The second behavioral type, suicidal behavior, is the final

aggregated result of all the symptoms of BPD inhabiting the individual's mind that might ultimately lead them to believe death to be a better option over the life they are currently living. Not all self-harm leads to death, though. Most people with BPD end up hurting themselves with no intention of suicide because they only need an outlet for all the pain and frustration building up within themselves. Nevertheless, it is regrettable that certain situations lead some people to act in such ways.

Moving on to the justifications for these situations, what exactly triggers these behaviors? For the person suffering from BPD, it could be anything unpleasant for them; the trigger could be anything from a minor comment to something as big as a traumatic incident. For example, the threat of a loved one separating from the individual could trigger their fear of abandonment, leading to impulsive and destructive behavior. A rough patch in one's relationship could act as a trigger to some people, while a troublesome incident could trigger others. In other words, triggers are respective to each individual, and we can only understand these triggers only if we fully understand our close ones with BPD. However, these triggers are most often led by the other symptoms of BPD. Fear and unstable relationships, such as in the previous examples, brew anger within persons, potentially lead to them hurt themselves.

Starting with anger issues, explosive anger is described as borderline rage, which happens when the individual is out of touch with reality. The angered response people with BPD usually exhibit is deemed inappropriate for the occasion that triggered it. They are often seen as having exaggerated, and their reactions might even appear selfish or manipulative. However, people with BPD are often misunderstood, and it is difficult to understand their situation.

Their disorder is often misdiagnosed, and incorrect methods to deal with them only worsen their condition. Their emotional range is high to the extent that these people usually take most things too seriously. Their reactions are a result of their sensitive thought process. But here is the deal; it is okay if a person is too sensitive. It is not necessarily a bad thing. However, it would be ideal for the individuals to learn how to handle their reactions better. An intense episode of anger is almost always associated with a dysregulation of emotions. People with BPD need to identify what methods help them return to the baseline and take back control over themselves.

In the previous chapter on stability, we have already given some tips on how people with BPD can implement it in their lives and how it will be beneficial in the long term. Often, these individuals come to their loved ones in the hope of receiving help. However, sometimes, they get told things that have the exact opposite effect. Therefore, we will give some pointers on things that one should never say to people with BPD. These tips might even help you deal with people suffering from other mental conditions.

Some phrases that are often heard spoken by people with BPD might sound like the following, "I'm having a hard time," or "I'm too depressed to act or think straight." If you've ever heard them, these are cries for help. If someone with BPD comes up to you and confesses these things, they probably want you to help them get through their torturous day. They would like you to acknowledge their feelings and make them feel validated for the emotions they are going through.

The incorrect way to go about this would be to compare their situation with your own experience or those of others.

But comparisons are never beneficial for anybody in, no matter what situation they are in, and especially if that a person is sensitive and mentally dealing with too many emotions. Instead of the comparison, it would be better if you only lent an ear. Sometimes, simply hearing the other person out can help their situation immensely.

Another big no in the list of things not to say to a person with BPD is telling them off for thinking about the past or asking them to stop doing it. Their past is what has brought them into this situation in the first place. They cannot stop thinking about it or escape from it simply because you told them to. It is much more complex than that. Stating this would insinuate that you do not understand where they are coming from, which is bound to worsen their situation. Do not invalidate their feelings or their experiences. It will have the opposite effect to what you intend.

Moving on to self-harm, we would like to first say that this is a sensitive topic that perhaps most people do not understand. Those who do not engage in self-harm will probably be incapable of comprehending how the person who gets these urges feels. If you are one of these persons, even though it is understandable on your part, we strongly advise you to keep your thoughts to yourselves. Expressing that you do not understand the other person with these urges will only invalidate their feelings, eventually leading the individual to engage in more severe self-mutilation, which could be potentially hazardous. Along with these actions, these people with BPD also harbor feelings of guilt for the activities they are engaging in.

The worst possible thing a person could say to another who contributes to self-harm is that they are doing so for attention. However, as we already mentioned in the second chapter, which covered self-harm, no individual hurts themselves to gain the attention of others. Instead, these people try to hide their scars to not attract attention towards them.

Self-mutilation is challenging to overcome, so if you are reading this because you do self-harm, we advise you to seek a professional for help. The doctors' job is to help you when you cannot help yourself. They will mainly be using methods such as CBT and DBT mentioned in the previous chapter, along with mayhap medication, that will help you regulate your emotions. For those reading to help their loved ones, please make sure you are there for them and help them take the therapy that they need. It will help them immensely and prevent their mental condition from worsening.

CHAPTER 8
PERSONAL RELATIONSHIPS

This chapter is perhaps the most important of this entire book. We will now deal with problems that people with BPD encounter in their relationships and how they could deal with their partners or children and friends to help them understand their situation. It will also briefly touch on how a person who does not suffer from this disorder can help someone in their life who is currently going through this journey.

While the inner turmoil within a person with BPD is exceptionally challenging to deal with, the final blow these people must suffer is the dent that this disorder leaves on their relationships. Starting with fear deeply rooted in the hearts of individuals with BPD makes them act out in ways that would annoy the people they consider close. For example, a fear of abandonment of family members or friends makes these people behave in more suspicious ways. They already are afraid somebody will eventually leave, so they start doubting their every move, driving them further away. This scenario is usually observed between partners; an individual with BPD who fears their partner will leave them will be curious about their whereabouts and may even accuse them of acts they have not committed.

Another example is when people with BPD push their friends away or even make them leave. One way they can do this is by saying hurtful things. While these cases are unjust on the ones at the receiving end, they need to understand where these people are getting their thoughts from in the first place. We suggest trying to find the root cause of the fear within them. For instance, a traumatic incident can lead people with BPD to believe that no one in their life will stay there forever. Understand that this is their way of defending themselves from the hurt that they have previously experienced. Instead of letting them act based on their fear, reassure them that they are essential to you and that life would be better with them in it. Convince them that their anxiety is misplaced, but while doing so, do not invalidate their feelings of fear. As mentioned previously, invalidation of their feelings may lead them to distance themselves further from you.

The fear people with BPD experience heightens their emotional range. They become more sensitive to the comments thrown their way. Keep in mind that even though friends joke amongst themselves, you might always be aware that certain seemingly harmless banter can hurt someone else's feelings. In situations like these, it is not easy to decipher whether you have said the wrong thing. The only thing you can do is to let your friend, partner, or child know that they can talk to you about the things you have said that might have unintentionally hurt them. Listen to them, understand them, and identify which topics are more sensitive to them.

Once you have a rough idea of which subjects are more delicate to them, make it a point to refrain from joking about them in the future. By following these steps, you will be indirectly showing them that you are aware of their feelings towards some particular things and that you respect that. Make sure that they know that whatever is important to them is also important to you. That will help them realize that you genuinely care for them.

Do not by any means make them feel as if they are "too sensitive." That is a phrase often used by people that do not understand the individual suffering. What might not be a big deal to you could mean the world to someone else; the importance of a matter, irrespective of what it is, is entirely subjective. Do not tell anyone how they should and should not feel about something. That will only make them feel guilty for dramatizing and drawing attention towards themselves, which is precisely the opposite of what they want.

On the other hand, some people with BPD have a tendency to act more clingy with those they are close to and love. They act particularly needy whenever they sense any hint of their loved one abandoning them, even if it's not there. However, just the same way the fear of abandonment makes people with BPD push their partners away, it is possible that the fear envelopes them and makes them start to act in a way that might even push their loved ones away.

These people may be more prone to stalking their partners and divulging their personal space. They tend to behave dramatically and want to part of every aspect of their partner's life. They almost seem mad with frenzy. But many times, they do not realize that they may be crossing a boundary with their behavior. Looking at it from the receiving end, if one's partner is invading their privacy, they are put in a real tough spot. You cannot let them continue with their behavior. However, telling them to outright stop might bring about the opposite effect. The most appropriate way to handle this situation would be to listen to them and the reasons for their behavior. Then ask them to listen to you and your difficulties regarding the situation they have placed you in.

Besides verbal comfort in such situations, one can also offer physical comfort to people with BPD. For example, some people are not good with their words. They are incapable of expressing their thoughts and emotions adequately. In such cases, these people usually opt for physical touch as a means to communicate; a simple touch, such as a hand on the shoulder or a pat on the back, does the job of telling someone that you are there for them and that you understand them will work perfectly. Likewise, holding another's hand or hugging them may be your way of transmitting your feelings to them. The possibility of its effectiveness is high as physical touch is a ubiquitous love language among the masses.

However, despite taking this approach is quite understandable and thoughtful on your part, it may not always be welcome by the person on the receiving end. For example, even though physical touch may symbolize love and affection for someone, for another person, it may hint at danger or even give rise to unpleasant memories. Keep in mind that most mental health disorders are born out of abuse, most of which occurs in the form of physical or sexual violence. In such cases, physical touch will most definitely not be appreciated by the recipient. Instead, it will have the exact opposite effect, acting as a trigger and possibly making that person believe that you, too, are an enemy.

To avoid these events from occurring, it is better to let the person suffering initiate these physical gestures. Once an individual with BPD reaches out to you in the form of these gestures, you may then continue to express yourself the appropriate way, depending on the situation. For example, they may ask for a hug, hold your hand or lean on you for support. All of these actions indicate that they trust you and that you physical contact from your end will be accepted. Remember, it is important to respect boundaries.

At times, people with BPD realize that those around them are recognizing their symptoms and behavior. Unfortunately, these people with BPD use this to their advantage to get out of unwanted situations. For instance, they may sometimes get so overwhelmed by their moods that they may need to take time off from their daily routine. For adults, this could mean getting out of work, while for children and teenagers, it could even mean abusing from their disorder to skip school or college. Eventually, this will strongly impact the individual's career and educational life, possibly even affecting their work and social circles. Even though it might seem like a good way of escaping, it is clearly a terrible approach. Individuals with BPD should genuinely try to get out of their misery, work towards their betterment, and establish honest relationships with their colleagues and classmates.

The disorder should not be used as a scapegoat for one's bad behavior. Even though BPD leads people to act on impulse, they are responsible for their actions once they acknowledge their disorder and the emotions that come with it. They should try to work towards their recovery instead of actively manipulating the situation and using their symptoms as a weapon. It is unfair to both themselves and those trying to help them.

If you are diagnosed with BPD, you should not make use of your symptoms as an excuse to gain pity you for no reason. If other persons, especially your close ones, realize that you are trying to gain their mercy or get out of tricky situations, they will most probably consider it as manipulation. Do not give people a chance to turn their backs on you when they have come so far solely to help you. That is how relationships are ruined.

CHAPTER 9
STRESS MANAGEMENT

In previous chapters, we discussed common coping mechanisms and social methods to steer away from the harmful aspects of BPD. Finally, we are at the part where we teach you a significant pillar of recovery: stress management. While coping mechanisms overlap with managing stress, our focus will be more inclined towards long-term habit building to reduce stress on a larger scale.

First of all, we need to address that a mindset shift is necessary. Not all forms of stress are harmful. Without some form of stress or challenges in life, existence can be very dull and meaningless. Therefore, the tips given below give you the tools that you need to navigate through the waves of pressure, but they will not entirely eliminate it.

Most of these changes will significantly help you deal with emotional dysregulation, stress, self-discipline, and motivation in the long term. Having well-reinforced positive habits is a core bedrock of stability in life, seizing opportunity, and chasing your goals. Think about it, every great leader or individual you ever read about in a book or newspaper has been touted as someone who built productive habits that led them far in the pursuit of success while keeping their internal selves solid and stable in the hardest of times. You may think, "But I'm no leader. I just want to get better." But here is the thing; you are the leader of your story. It is you who will lead yourself through the obstacles of stress.

Now, you must be wondering how you could start building stress management habits and where to even begin with in the first place. This is why we will start with the best and most basic thing: quality sleep. Lack of quality sleep is strongly associated with other symptoms of BPD. We will even go as far as to state that poor sleep worsens further prominent symptoms of the disorder such as emotional dysregulation, mental stress, internal strife, and negative overthinking during the night. In some extreme cases, insomnia even leads to suicidal thoughts. Daytime functioning, which in the case of BPD may already be impaired, is also further exacerbated.

But then, you might ask, "What even is good sleep?" The National Sleep Foundation states that, as an adult, you should get between 7 to 9 hours of sleep every night; any less than that will reduce functioning, especially if you get even less than 6 hours of sleep. Hence, if you are not sleeping enough, you are impeding your recovery from BPD as quality sleep is the gateway to productivity, feeling emotionally stable, and building habits. Hence, without feeling energized and emotionally stable after a long night's sleep, how will you manage to conquer the day and accomplish your goals?

If you are suffering in this regard, the first thing you can try is to avoid any coffee or alcohol near bedtime hours.

These substances will only lead to you be more awake, alert, on edge, and in the case of liquor, more prone to needless rumination and negative thinking. Even though alcohol can help you fall asleep with ease, it will interfere with your sleep quality, which is why you should avoid it entirely.

Another tactic that can be used alongside this is setting up a routine where you go to bed early, organize your day-to-day schedule, and avoid staying on your phone late at night. This is a solid contributor to insomnia because the blue light emitted from your cellphone fools your brain into thinking that daylight is emanating from the phone. Therefore, it disrupts your regular sleep cycle, making it harder to fall asleep. You can make use of a blue light filter or switch your phone to night mode, but it is not as effective as ditching your phone altogether during the late hours. Try to stop using any phones or electronic media at least an hour before you plan on going to bed.

It might also be beneficial to turn the air conditioner on to make your bedroom cooler. This will make sleeping easier as the cool air helps relax the body. Another possible remedy to counter ongoing sleep deprivation can include the consumption of peppermint tea after midday so that caffeine does not interfere during your bedtime later during the day. You may also find luck with mobile applications that play relaxing and meditative music that can also help induce sleep.

Another approach that you might consider is planned sleep deprivation under a doctor's supervision, the same one that Joey practiced. Yes, we, too, are huge fans of the Friends TV show. For example, pull an all-nighter, force yourself to stay up one entire day, and then sleep at the desired bedtime as per your goals. Then, you can go to bed early and wake up earlier when the sun rises, thereby fixing your sleep routine.

Remember to not stress over setting your sleep cycle too early. Instead, take baby steps; start by going to bed thirty minutes before usual and gradually shifting your bedtime earlier over the course of weeks. It might even be a good idea to invest in a better mattress because our sleep problems often stem from an uneven or lumpy mattress. Similarly, you could buy a new pillow that may give more comfort compared to an old one.

Physical activity can also be beneficial in helping you control your inner self better. Our ancestors lived by way of hunting and training to master their physical prowess concerning their senses. Therefore, it is no secret that many people find themselves within their most primal part, which is to exert their limits physically. Research has proven that physical activity such as working out, boxing, swimming, or riding a bicycle leads to a fast decline in depression. Conversely, it has been reported that teens who live a sedentary lifestyle are much more likely to ponder over suicide or self-harm. The more idle one, the more likely they will act upon negative thoughts.

Exercise will stimulate you physically and alleviate your other depressive symptoms such as anxiety, tension, laziness, or fatigue. It allows stronger emotional regulation and navigation of thoughts in their place. Those obsessive thoughts that keep bugging you day in and day out will grow weaker in their intensity as you physically exert yourself and get pumped up with adrenaline. This significant benefit of calming yourself post-exercise is due to a decrease in cortisol.

These gains are an excellent reason for getting a gym membership or joining a sports club. Doing so will allow you to expand your social circle by engaging with other fitness enthusiasts who can further motivate you to keep pushing beyond your physical limits at the same time. In addition, the benefits such as increased muscle mass, reduced body fat, and greater central nervous system coordination resulting from weight training will give you a massive boost in self-confidence.

People who start their fitness journeys report lifestyle changes in various aspects of their life as well. These include the increased likelihood of avoiding junk food, which is excellent for your emotional stability, improved sleep quality due to increased hormonal balance, and an increased sense of self-worth. You will no longer be prey to thoughts of not being enough for other people because you will feel fantastic improving your physical performance, whether it is getting stronger, faster, leaner, or fitter. In addition, the increased self-confidence will help you in pursuing new friendships and new relationships.

If you cannot afford to join a gym or sports club, make a habit of going out for a brisk walk outside, even if it is only for ten minutes daily. You do not have to start an all-out extreme routine from day one. In fact, please do not do that because you will burn yourself out. Start small and gradually build your way up. The key is not to try very hard; rather, it is to remain consistent and make it a part of your life. As long as you do any physical activity daily, you will make progress.

If, after trying vigorous exercise, you did not enjoy it, there are still some great alternatives. You could opt for other activities that are more catered towards stimulating your mental focus and senses instead of your physical strength. These activities can be a very cost-effective option, such as in the case of yoga.

Yoga is an excellent method for tackling stress and emotional dysregulation as it primarily focuses on physical poses and deep, controlled breathing techniques accompanied by meditation. Compared to sports or weight training, yoga is very low in risk, low in cost, and very accessible. Benefits of yoga include increased mental clarity, improved respiration, lowered heart rate, improved blood pressure, and more feelings of well-being. All you need is a single mat to place on the floor. In fact, you can even do without out in the beginning! Just start in your living room if you want.

Another method you could try your hand is martial arts! Yeah, this is one of the most incredible things you could try. Its benefits overlap with those of physical exercise and yoga combined. Plus, imagine how cool it telling people you can do Jujitsu or Krav- maga would be!

The way you manage stress is also influenced by your diet. After all, a man is what he eats. Whatever you consume will internally lead to either well-being or contribute to feelings of illness and imbalance. Negative emotions and urges for escapism further exacerbate sugar cravings, binge eating, or even episodes of skipping meals entirely. When we are stressed, the human body secretes more cortisol, which is basically a stress hormone. As a result, you crave fatty, sugary, and salty foods because your brain thinks that the body requires more fuel to counter the perceived stress threat. But by doing so, this craving is made even worse since stress might also lower our metabolic rate and cause weight gain.

As mentioned earlier in this book, you should identify your stress triggers and avoid extreme actions such as binge eating or not eating at all. One of the best things you can do to prevent sugar cravings and urges for unhealthy sodas or alcohol is to increase your daily water intake. Keeping yourself well hydrated will reduce cravings for sodas or high sugar drinks, thereby preventing weight gain. Water will also keep you feeling refreshed and make your skin glow in less than 24 hours of appropriate hydration. Now isn't that a great incentive to drink more water?

It is also a good idea to have healthy, ready-made snacks available on the get-go for when you might feel hungry. It is always an even better idea to prepare meals in advance so that you do not succumb to unnecessary cravings when you are stressed, especially when you least expect it. Apart from saving money, which could also contribute to reducing your stress, it can counter the likelihood of ordering fast food or grabbing munchies and cookies from the store. You can even plan to include vegetables and fruits, which are excellent carbohydrate sources. Keeping your meal plans too simple or cooking something complex will induce more stress and initiate a triggering response. Therefore, include fruits, vegetables, pieces of chicken breast, or anything minor maintenance.

Your focus regarding the contents of your meals should prioritize complex carbs that promote the release of the hormone that makes one feel good, i.e., Serotonin. That means that whole grains, pieces of bread, portions of pasta, and oatmeal are your best friends. These are also excellent sources of healthy, non-fattening carbohydrates, which will be beneficial for muscle building if you are working out.

That brings us to protein sources. You should focus on including them in your meals to remain healthy, lose fat, and get into better shape. Protein sources include fish, meat, chicken, almonds, chickpeas, and milk. Healthy fat sources such as avocados and fish should be included too. Apart from these, you might even invest some interest in supplements. Any nutritional deficiencies you may possess can be dealt with by purchasing tablets from a pharmacy. You can specifically target stress by consuming lemon balm pills, which are basically mints that reduce anxiety. Or you could also opt for Omega-3-fatty acids, which are heavily concentrated in fish meat. Another thing you can purchase is Ashwagandha, a herb used in Indian societies to treat stress and anxiety.

Another prominent contributor to our stresses of life in this modern age can also be poor time management. When one has a long day without any preplanned schedule to break down his goals into smaller segments, they may face tremendous stress. Here, stress presents itself as a combination of impulsivity, agitated mood, emotional dysregulation, etc. By planning out your schedule beforehand, you can give yourself more time for self-care and to manage symptoms of stress such as hunger. You can rely on premade meals to lift your spirits, fit in a workout to make yourself feel better, or sleep before any strenuous work to be better prepared.

When planning your schedule beforehand, keep in mind that it is best to have a realistic vision. You may ask your therapist or friend for their input when working on this. Take a piece of paper, a diary, or a calendar and write your plans for the days ahead. Include meal times, workout plans, showers, or anything that you plan to do for leisure to de-stress. Planning is essential as you will know what to expect and will therefore be less likely to succumb to temptations of binge eating, self-harm, or not doing anything at all in response to increased stress. Also, allow a certain degree of flexibility for your day so that you have other backup goals planned out in the case of not being able to carry out these activities.

Apart from managing internal factors such as diet and

sleep, you should also surround yourself with stress reducers. Using scented candles to light up your room or workspace is an excellent example of this. This method is called aromatherapy and has been proven to improve one's sleep. In addition, essential oils can work wonders on our internal selves and de-stress as they remind our brains of nature. You should mainly invest in products consisting of Lavender, Neroli, Vetiver, Orange blossom, or Geranium.

It is crucial to view content that makes you feel better during your leisure time, such as comedy, romantic comedies, action, adventure, or satire. Also, watching anything funny or sharing hilarious memes with a friend should do the trick of removing stress for the time being. In fact, laughter and humor themselves are potent remedies for stress.

It is essential to surround yourself with positive people with whom you do not have to guess second anything you might want to say or express; you deserve that much. It would be best if you were more expressive physically. Physical intimacy, touch, and sexual and intimate desires are very humane experiences that can lower one's stress. Do not forget to hug your partner between day-to-day activities. Research has proven that forms of positive physical gestures like cuddling and hugging lower stress via the release of Oxytocin and reduced blood pressure.

Lastly, it is also essential to keep in mind that progress in the case of BPD is not going to be linear. The same applies to dealing with stress and forming anti-stress habits. While you may believe it is good to hold yourself up to high standards with little room for failure, you should know that this will, in turn, impede your progress. Instead, have a mindset where you recognize that even if you do slip up or fail to perform any task in your recovery, you are still moving forward. It is okay if you end up relapsing to binge eating or alcohol consumption. You must look at the bigger picture; merely being on this incredible journey deserves praise. Having guilt or shame will do more harm than good. Below we shall look at how to move on from setbacks because not being able to do so will further amplify the stress you tried to escape from in the first place.

Realize that a setback is an opportunity. Through this failure, analyze the series of events that led you here. In turn, this will allow you to learn how each trigger can lead to a relapse. Viewing these failures this way will prevent you from further spiraling down into self-destructive cycles as now your subconscious cannot rationalize, "I have already failed once. So what is the point of recovery? I might as well just give up now."

Spend some time reflecting on any setback by asking yourself the important questions, such as "Was I getting lazy or overconfident with my recovery tasks?" or "Was I skipping my therapy sessions?" or "Was I viewing the world and myself in a negative light recently?" The answers to these questions should be relevant in your next therapy session; your therapist should be able to discuss and help you get right back on track, offering you a sympathetic voice for reassurance. Be honest with yourself and also with your therapist. It is also a bad idea to pretend as if your setback never occurred. This behavior itself is a form of escapism, a willful ignorance. Instead, it is an excellent idea to write down the reasons for your failure and how you can avoid repeating the same mistakes in the future. This method will help you accept what has happened and thereby allowing you to move on.

The guilt experienced after a step back can be a potent

reminder of why you want to change into a better version of yourself. However, if you do not take this approach, guilt can further destroy your progress by making you feel worse. Hence, try working on getting back to your anti-stress habits asap or do something healthy that you enjoy. Pick yourself back up, but also realize that you must have realistic expectations of this journey. It may be tempting to set high expectations to succeed in battling stress or the negativity associated with BPD. Still, these unrealistic expectations will only de-motivate you instead of preparing you for the long-term process. So if you are going through the effects of guilt after a step in the opposite direction, just relax. It is okay. You will be fine. Tomorrow is a new day.

CHAPTER 10
CONCLUSION

Congratulations, readers! You have made it to the end of the book. We would like to ask you to take a deep breath and exhale it out. You are victorious in finishing this book on Borderline Personality Disorder with more knowledge about this mental health disorder than before. You know all the things associated with this disorder and how you can help yourself if you have BPD or are suspicious of having it. If you were reading to help someone and strengthen your relationship with them, you now know various ways of doing that.

In some instances, the symptoms of BPD may present themselves as extremes. But remember, all of these problems have a solution. Other than the self-help methods offered to you throughout this book, it would be best if you also underwent therapy. A doctor is more able to diagnose a mental health disorder than a self-help book. He will also be more equipped and capable of aiding your condition and leading you back on the road to normalcy.

Do not hesitate to ask for help. Doing so is a brave act in itself. Be sure to contact the local BPD hotline for more information on this disorder!

We part ways here. All we have to say now is that you do not need to be afraid. Things will only go uphill from here.

We wish you the best of luck on your journey!

Thank you so much for reading!

If you feel you have benefited from this book or it has provided you with value of some sort then we would love to get your feedback via an honest Amazon review!

Printed in Great Britain
by Amazon